Music
Mind
Movement

TUNING IN

Practical Psychology
for
Musicians
who are
Teaching, Learning and Performing

Handbook and Home Study Course
by
Lucinda Mackworth-Young

First published in 2000

by MMM Publications

Second impression 2002

Third impression 2003

Fourth impression 2005

Fifth impression 2010

Sixth impression and digital edition 2017

ISBN 0-9539485-0-1

British Library Cataloguing in Publication Data

A CIP catalogue record for this title is available from the British Library

"We perceive the interplay of forces in two basic modes, the holistic, intuitive mode of the right hemisphere and the unconscious; and the linear, analytic, conscious mode of the left hemisphere. Communication between conscious and unconscious and through the latter to the spirit, depends on an openness to both modes of awareness. Verbal concepts must be translated into symbols and images; unconscious images must be brought to the light of consciousness. Through open communication we can become attuned to the primal, ecstatic union that is the force of creation".

Miriam Symos, *The Spiral Dance,* 1979

Foreword

Tuning In is for instrumental and singing teachers and performers. It is relevant to all teachers who teach individually or in small groups, whether their pupils are young or mature, beginners or advanced students.

It draws on psychology, psychotherapy and counselling skills and a wealth of practical music teaching and performing experience, so that musicians can deepen their awareness and understanding of the many processes involved in music teaching, learning and performing, and enhance and enrich their skills.

In particular, it seeks to spell out the intuitive processes that all good teachers and performers use, so that these processes can be more fully appreciated and then used with conscious intent, to greater effect.

It is set out experientially. That is, as far as possible, the reader first connects with his or her own experiences through the exercises given, and then the underlying principles are explained. In this way the psychology feels both directly relevant and easy to grasp.

Practical suggestions for enhancing teaching, learning and performing arise out of the psychological understanding and are described in every chapter. Most chapters end with a Summary and Practical Checklist. All chapters allow space for personal reflection and a personal practical checklist.

It can be read straight through, used as a resource, or studied as a course.

For clarity, the teacher is referred to as "she" and the pupil as "he".

Acknowledgements

This book is grounded in many years' experience in both music and psychology.

Of particular significance in the experience, and so in the book, are the following,

to whom I give many grateful thanks:

All of my music teachers, especially

Dorothy Hunt, Olive Hayward, Marjorie McAdams, Colin Bradbury,

and Alfred Kitchin and Joan Barker from Trinity College of Music.

Norman Worrall (The Institute of Education, London University), Margot Waddell (The Tavistock Clinic, London), Yiannis Arzoumanides (The London School of Counselling) and Margot Sunderland (The Institute for Arts in Therapy and Education, London) whose educational and psychological courses were so illuminating.

All of my pupils and students, past and present, from whom I have learnt and continue to learn so much, and the many professional musicians who have attended my courses and workshops, or sought private consultation.

Finally, I would like to thank Naomi Hymes, Stephanie John, Barbara Lloyd and Jennie Parke Matheson for the photographs of workshops for the front cover. Also, Katy Waters, Angela Mackworth-Young and Ryan Morison and the team at Erudition whose help with editing this book has been invaluable

Introduction

When we learn we can only start from where we are. From where we are we find ourselves drawn to sources (teachers, books, courses) which evoke in us the response: *"Yes! This is what I want!"*.

The source is attractive because it is responding to a process we have already begun within ourselves, it promises to answer questions we have already asked within ourselves. It feeds the hunger we have already felt, and we lap it up eagerly, wanting more. Should we then find that it doesn't nourish us, perhaps because it's too much, or because it's indigestible, our appetite wanes.

Understanding and being able to handle these and many other emotional and psychological processes in music teaching, learning and performing is what this book is all about.

To help you get the most out of the following pages:

> First, think and then write in the box below what you enjoy in your teaching or performing and what you feel good at. (If you are not yet teaching or performing, think and write what attracts you to them: what would you *like* to enjoy and feel good at):

> Spend a minute or two reflecting on and enjoying what you have just written. Allow your enjoyable and successful feelings to strengthen your belief in yourself and in your teaching or performing.

It is only if we feel sufficiently secure in what we *are* doing that we feel able to open up, look around and consider other points of view and methods in case they may enhance what we are already doing.

Now, think and write what you would like to enjoy more or do better and what you would like your pupils to enjoy more and do better. (If you are not already teaching or performing, omit this box and read on):

Now that you have identified your goals you can more easily find the resources that can help you. By looking at the Table of Contents and glancing through, you will have a better idea of whether or not this book is for you.

I very much hope that it is, and that you enjoy it,

Lucinda Mackworth-Young

September, 2010

Contents

Chapter One: Emotions in Education ... 11
The Pupil's Emotional Experience and the Role of Teacher ... 11
Beginnings: Heightened emotional intensity ... 16
Learning Anxiety: Not being able to do it ... 16
Keying in to "Inner Child": Roots in infancy ... 17
Teacher as Parent: Caregiver and Critic ... 19
Internalising Parents and Teachers: ... 19
Transference: from parents and other previous authority figures ... 21
Transference: from the Ideal Parent ... 22
Transference: onto future music lessons and the whole world of music ... 22
Becoming Independent: Strengthening the pupil's "Inner Carer" ... 22
Endings ... 24
Chapter Two: Learning and Teaching ... 29
Teaching for Learning ... 29
Understanding Learning ... 32
Understanding Teaching ... 32
Emotional Engagement: Wanting to learn ... 32
Holistic (right-brained) and Step-by-Step (left-brained) Skills ... 33
Aural, Kinaesthetic and Intellectual/Visual Skills ... 34
Unity and Control ... 37
Whole Body Skills ... 38
Teaching Styles ... 40
The Key is in Success ... 43
Chapter Three: Emotions, Motivation and Practice ... 47
Understanding Motivation ... 51
Accessing Pupils' Feelings ... 51
Common Feelings Underlying Lack of Practice ... 55
Practical Suggestions to Motivate Pupils to Practise ... 55
When Pupils *Still* Don't Practice ... 59

Chapter Four: Maintaining Positive Energy ... 62
Dealing with Negative Feeling ... 63
Understanding Positive Energy ... 65
Being Aware of Energy ... 72
Using Countertransference ... 72
Difficulties in Recognising Pupils' Negative Feelings ... 73
Common Causes of Negative Energy in Pupils ... 73
Being Aware of Our Own Feelings and their Effects on Pupils ... 74
Common Causes of Negative Energy in Teachers and the Effects on Pupils ... 77
Maintaining Positive Energy: Practical Suggestions ... 78
Dealing with Negative Feeling ... 80
Parting ... 84
Chapter Five: Making Music Now ... 88
Practical Activities to Have Fun and Raise Energy ... 88
Making Music Now ... 88
Moving ... 88
Playing Together ... 88
Improvising ... 89
Graphic Notation ... 90
Chapter Six: Group Teaching ... 93
Exploring How to Teach in Groups ... 94
Advantages of Group Music Lessons ... 94
Overlapping Lessons ... 94
Sibling Rivalry ... 95
Emotionally Demanding Behaviour ... 95
Differing Abilities ... 96
Chapter Seven: Parents ... 99
Teachers, Pupils and Parents ... 101
Understanding Pupils and Parents ... 101
Understanding Teachers and Parents ... 103
Establishing and Maintaining a Working Relationship ... 104
Dealing with Difficulty ... 106
Chapter Eight: Age-Related Learning Guide ... 112
Summary of Chapters One to Seven ... 113

Chapter Nine: Performance 116
Anxiety, Communication and Safety 117
Understanding Performing 121
Understanding Performance Anxiety 121
Understanding What the Audience and Examiners Want 121
Unhelpful Societal Notions: "Show off!" "Who do you think you are?" 123
The "Inner Parent": "Inner Critic" or "Inner Carer" 123
The "Inner Critic" 123
The "Inner Carer" 124
Gender Differences 124
Balancing the "Inner Carer and "Inner Critic" 124
The "Free Inner Child" 124
Connecting with the "Deep Self" and with the Audience 125
Positive Energy 125
Practical Suggestions for Preparation for Performance: 127
Emotional, Physical and Mental 127
Emotional Preparation for Performance 127
Physical and Mental Preparation for Performance: 130
Just Before the Performance 132
Enjoying Performing 133
Chapter Ten: Action Research 135
Understanding Action Research 136
Choose a Topic 136
Select your Pupils 138
Define your Aims 138
Design your Method 138
Do the Research 140
Write up your Results 140
Draw your Conclusions and make Recommendations for further study 140
Example of a Teacher's Plan for Action Research 141
The Questionnaire 142
Afterword 144
References and Recommended Reading 145

Chapter One: Emotions in Education

The Pupil's Emotional Experience and the Role of Teacher

"Feelings which we usually relegate to infants and very young children, are indeed ubiquitous ... anxieties continue to exist to some degree in all of us throughout life. Knowing about them from within ourselves increases our perceptiveness and understanding of others."

Isca Saltzberger-Wittenberg,

The Emotional Experience of Learning and Teaching, 1983

EXERCISE WORKSHEET: EXPLORING PUPILS' EMOTIONS

Answer the questions below, recalling your feelings in individual/small group instrumental or vocal music lessons with three different teachers:

(a) The first teacher you had (at primary school age?)

(b) The second or third teacher you had (at secondary school age?)

(c) A teacher you had aged 18+

What were your feelings on going to your first lesson with each teacher? What did you hope for? What did you dread? What did you expect? What did you need?

(a)

(b)

(c)

What were your first impressions of each teacher and each teaching environment? How did they affect your feelings?

(a)

(b)

(c)

What were the positive feelings experienced in lessons? What caused them and how did they affect you in lessons and practice?

(a)

(b)

(c)

What were the negative emotions experienced in lessons? What caused them and how did they affect you in lessons and practice?

(a)

(b)

(c)

What did you expect in terms of encouragement, praise or criticism from each teacher? Why? How did your expectations affect your experience?

(a)

(b)

(c)

If things weren't going well for you how did you express yourself: through words? Tone of voice? Silence? Actions (e.g. lack of practice)? Body language? Or feeling?

(a)

(b)

(c)

What do you think each teacher felt about you and your ability? How was this conveyed: through words? Tone of voice? Silence? Actions? Body language? Or feeling? And how did it affect your learning?

(a)

(b)

(c)

What did each teacher do or what could have been done to help engender positive feelings?

(a)

(b)

(c)

As a professional music teacher you could be regarded as a survivor of the system. The chances are that you had a positive experience throughout most of your musical education. It is less usual for people who had predominantly negative experiences as pupils to become professional, but where there is talent and a real love of the subject this can happen.

> You may now find it illuminating to answer the same questions (set out below) in relation to a subject or activity that you disliked and wanted to give up:

What were your feelings on going to your first lesson with each teacher? What did you hope for? What did you dread? What did you expect? What did you need?

(a)

(b)

(c)

What were your first impressions of each teacher and each teaching environment? How did they affect your feelings?

(a)

(b)

(c)

What were the positive feelings experienced in lessons? What caused them and how did they affect you in lessons and practice?

(a)

(b)

(c)

What were the negative emotions experienced in lessons? What caused them and how did they affect you in lessons and practice?

(a)

(b)

(c)

What did you expect in terms of encouragement, praise or criticism from each teacher? Why? How did your expectations affect your experience?

(a)

(b)

(c)

If things weren't going well for you how did you express yourself: through words? Tone of voice? Silence? Actions (e.g. lack of practice)? Body language? Or feeling?

(a)

(b)

(c)

What do you think each teacher felt about you and your ability? How was this conveyed: through words? Tone of voice? Silence? Actions? Body language? Or feeling? And how did it affect your learning?

(a)

(b)

(c)

What did each teacher do or what could have been done to help engender positive feelings?

(a)

(b)

(c)

Beginnings: Heightened emotional intensity

The beginning of anything new brings heightened emotional intensity, both excitement and fear. Like animals entering new territory, all our senses are on the alert as we hope to find what we seek, but fear danger. Even an excited pupil who is looking forward to learning will experience some fear, and for many pupils there will be a great deal of fear. Fear can be about finding the building or studio, being late, being welcomed and accepted by fellow pupils and, especially, being welcomed, accepted and appreciated by the teacher. Younger pupils may also be concerned about how long they'll be there, who will be collecting them or where they should go next, and whether they can find the bathroom without having to ask! But, as a general rule, the younger the pupil the more the excitement, and the older and more self-aware the pupil, the worse the fears. Any previous experience of the building, studio, fellow pupils or teacher can help to reduce fear.

First impressions

Owing to the heightened emotional intensity, first impressions of the studio and the teacher, whether typical or not, are both powerful and long lasting. A warm and welcoming first impression of the studio and teacher will evoke warm and welcomed feelings within the pupil and give him the belief that music is a safe and enjoyable place to be. The potency of these initial feelings will also help sustain him when, later, the going gets harder. It need hardly be added that an uncared for, cold or bleak first impression of a studio or an unwelcoming first impression of a teacher, may be equally powerful and make it very difficult for the pupil to feel either safety or enjoyment. It may even put him off music lessons for life.

Learning Anxiety: Not being able to do it

In addition to fears about the studio, fellow pupils and teacher, there may also be anxiety about learning itself. Usually well hidden, as it's not "cool" to show such feelings in our society, there is a fear of "not being able to do it", a fear of failing. Fearing not being able to do it and, worse, finding that he can't do it, may cause the pupil to feel very anxious and sometimes utterly overwhelmed with anxiety, as though he is falling apart or falling into a bottomless pit. It can literally feel *unbearable.*

This learning anxiety is exacerbated as the pupil not only has to learn, but has to learn in front of the teacher, the perceived authority. He not only fears not being able to do it, but he fears that he might be found wanting, and humiliated, annihilated or cast out.

Signs of anxiety

Common signs of learning anxiety include engaging the teacher in distracting chatter (especially at the beginning of lessons!), providing endless valid-sounding reasons for not practising, "forgetting" the music, arriving late or leaving early. Other signs are: seizing up, "going stupid", sitting in uncommunicative silence or running away in mind: *"I'm not listening!"* or in body, either by begging to be allowed to give up or, simply, by not turning up.

The most common sign of learning anxiety is avoiding practice, or avoiding practising certain things (scales, difficult passages etc.). It can feel better not to *try* than to try and *fail.*

These anxious feelings, whether in lessons or practice, may seem out of all proportion to the actual situation. The adult learner, especially, may be aware that the intensity both of his fear of "not being able to do it" and of his need for the teacher's approval seems absurd, but yet he feels caught up in it. Why?

Keying in to "Inner Child": Roots in infancy

As we experience any emotion we cannot help but be keyed back into earlier experiences of the same emotion. So when did we first experience anxiety about "not being able to do it"?

In infancy.

To the infant, hunger, thirst, heat, cold or loneliness are intensely experienced. They are life threatening, but the infant is utterly unable to do anything about them by himself. He can only cry, and the cry expresses the way he feels. It can sound as though he feels overwhelmed with helplessness and terror, as though he feels he is falling apart or falling into a bottomless pit.

So, the feelings of anxiety experienced in education may seem out of all proportion to those warranted by the actual situation because they reawaken the similar but infinitely more profound feelings of utter helplessness and terror in the face of not-being-able-to-succeed experienced by the infant-within-the-pupil.

Simply by becoming a pupil, whether at the age of six or sixty-six, the pupil cannot help but key back, at some level, into his own inner infantile and early childhood emotions, his "Inner Child". He may easily feel anxiety and helplessness to the extent that "not being able to do it" is experienced as severely threatening. A matter of life and death.

In "Inner Child" the pupil then transfers onto the teacher the role of "Parent" having a seemingly out of proportion need for care and fear of criticism.

Understanding Pupils and Teachers

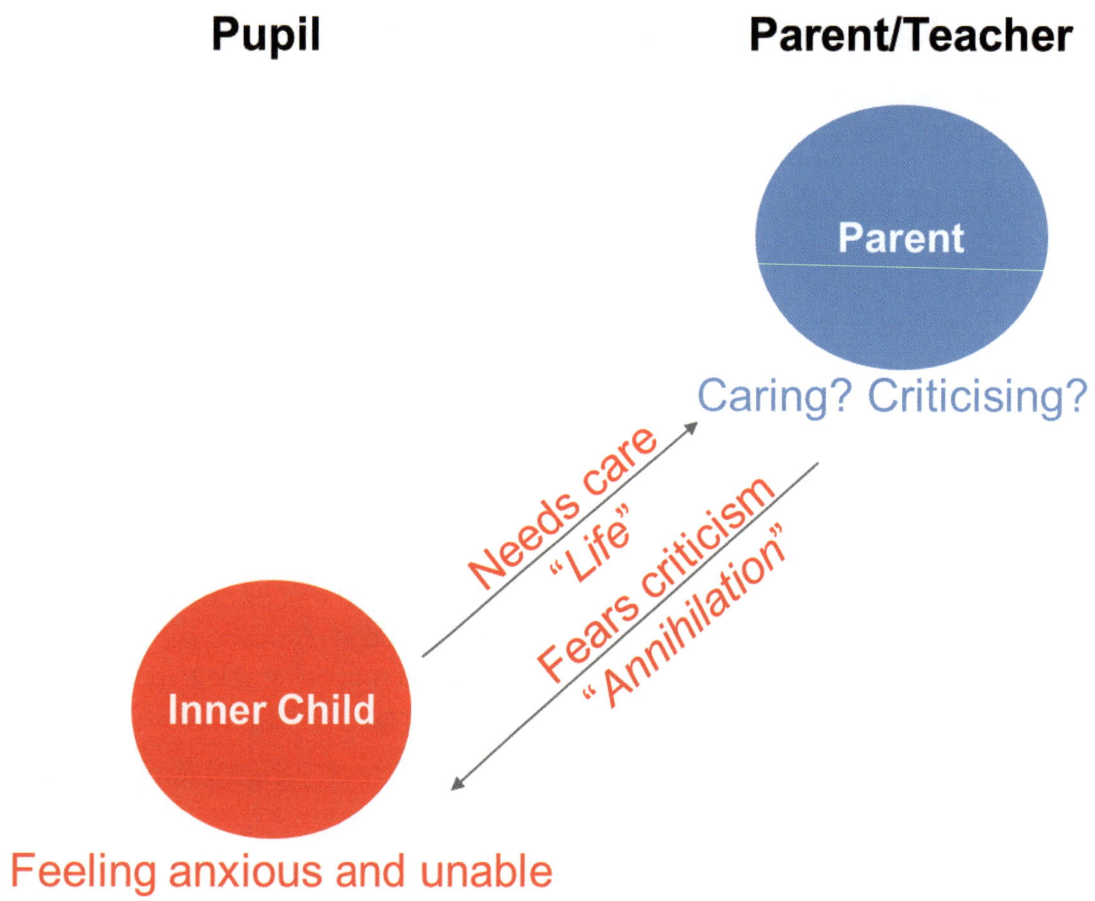

The pupil keys into ***Inner Child***, feeling anxious, fearing being "unable to do it", and transfers onto the teacher the role of ***Parent***, or ultimate authority figure, needing care and fearing criticism.

Teacher as Parent: Caregiver and Critic

The parental role is twofold, both nurturing *and* authoritative, or: Caregiving *and* Critical.

Teacher as Caregiver

In the same way that the infant depends on the parent to make him feel safe and secure, to contain his anxiety, *then* he can take in, feed and grow, so the pupil, at any age, depends on the teacher to make him feel safe and secure in her presence, recognise and contain any learning anxiety, *then* he can learn. Only if the pupil feels internally secure can he learn, because learning requires him to be prepared to open up to something new, to try and to risk failing.

Typically the mother contains her infant by wrapping her arms around him, bearing his anxious feelings and providing for his needs. In a similar way the pupil looks to the teacher to have her mind around him, bearing his anxious feelings and providing the emotional reassurance and practical help that he needs.

Teacher as Ultimate Authority or Critic

Just as to the helpless infant the parent is all powerful, knows everything and is always right so, through transference, there is a level at which the pupil believes the teacher is all powerful, knows everything and is right, especially where music and his ability are concerned. In being perceived as the Ultimate Authority in this way, the teacher has enormous power and significance in the eyes of the pupil.

Caregiver or Critic: Life Giver or Annihilator?

Just as through the quality of her care, the parent literally has the power of life or death, comfort or discomfort, over the helpless infant so, through transference and the quality of her care, the teacher has the power of musical life or death, comfort or discomfort over the pupil. Care, interest and appreciation from the parent is life giving, and conveys to the child that he matters and can succeed as a person, whereas neglect or disapproval can severely threaten both physical and emotional survival. Similarly, care, interest and appreciation from the teacher are musically life giving and convey to the pupil that he matters and can succeed as a musical person, whereas neglect or disapproval can severely threaten musical survival.

Internalising Parents and Teachers:

The “Inner Parent”: “Inner Carer” or “Inner Critic”

Whatever messages the pupil receives from parents or teachers, whether caring or critical, and however they are conveyed (whether through words, tone of voice, silences, actions, body language or feeling), he may then *internalise* so that they become what he believes about himself and says inside his head to himself daily. They become his "Inner Parent".

Thus, a child who receives care, approval and encouragement, receives positive messages about himself such as: *"You matter as a person"*, and: *"You can succeed"*. When internalised these messages then become: *"I matter as a person"*, and: *"I can succeed"*. This child then has a caring, supportive “Inner Parent” or, more simply, an “Inner Carer”.

On the other hand, a child who has not been so cared for and has perhaps even been persistently criticised, will have internalised critical messages such as: *"You're no good", "You'll never be good enough", "The others are much better than you", "You won't get anywhere"* and so have a critical "Inner Parent" or, an "Inner Critic".

In the same way, a pupil who receives care, approval and encouragement from the teacher will feel and then internalise: *"I matter as a musical person",* and *"I can succeed with music".* Or, if he feels more criticism than care he is more likely to internalise: *"I'm no good", "I'll never be good enough", "The others are much better than me", "I won't get anywhere".*

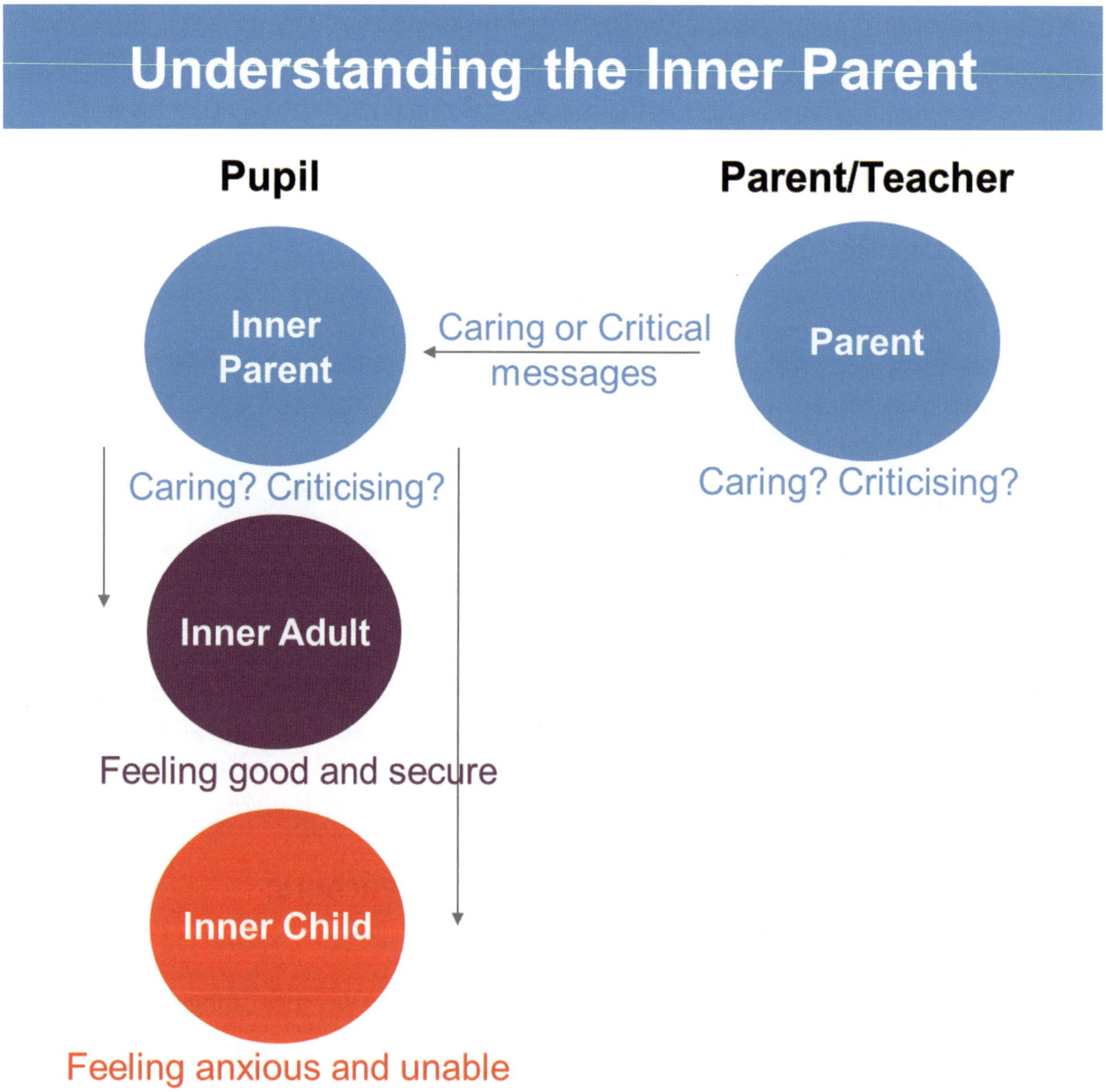

Pupils receive messages from parents and teachers about themselves and their behaviour which they may internalise to become what they say inside their own heads to themselves: their ***Inner Parent***.

The messages can be Caring and supportive, or Critical and undermining.

The need for the "Inner Carer" in learning

A strong "Inner Carer" is essential in learning. The "Inner Carer" is the inner resource which supports the pupil internally thus enabling him to be open and to sit with "not knowing" and the fear of "not being able to do it" while patiently working out what to do, how to do it and *trying* it. A critical *awareness* is necessary in alerting the pupil to quality and spurring work. But, if not balanced by the "Inner Carer", the "Inner Critic" destroys the pupil internally, resulting in increased learning anxiety, increased fear of the teacher and no internal resource, so that the pupil is unable to sit with and persist through difficulties, and gives up or runs away.

It must be borne in mind, though, that the pupil's internalisations are not, solely, the parents' or teachers' responsibility. Owing to differences in innate disposition (evident at or soon after birth), infants, children or pupils *elicit* different messages from parents and teachers and they also play an active part in accepting or rejecting them. Messages which resonate with the child's feeling and any existing internalisations are more likely to be accepted than those that don't.

Transference: from parents and other previous authority figures

By the time the pupil comes for music lessons he will have internalised a great deal from parents and other authority figures, previous teachers included, and have already developed an "Inner Parent", whether predominantly caring or critical. He will then *transfer* his experience onto the new music teacher *expecting* her to treat him as he has been treated before, and he may do this so compellingly that the teacher is actually provoked into behaving as the pupil expects. As a simple illustration of this, consider how your own response differs to a new pupil who enters with a smile, sure you'll be friendly (a positive transference from the "Inner Carer"), and one who enters with a fearful or hostile scowl, certain you'll find fault (a negative transference from the "Inner Critic").

Inevitably, pupils' transferences affect their *experience.* Pupils with a strong "Inner Carer" are more able to hear or feel and respond to our care, encouragement and appreciation than those without, because that is what they *expect.* Likewise, pupils with a strong "Inner Critic" may only be able to hear or feel criticism, whether or not we've said a word, because that is what *they* expect.

If conscious and verbalised, typical transferences could be, for example:

"My parents always praise my efforts so you will too" .

Or: *"My parents always criticise and think I'm not good enough, so you'll think that too".*

Or: *"My first teacher never allowed me to play what I wanted to play, so you won't either".*

Or: *"You look like Uncle John so you'll behave like him too".*

Many an initial antipathy from a pupil to a teacher can be explained in terms of a negative transference. If the teacher is aware of this and is persistently friendly and understanding in the face of it, it may well fall away.

Transference: from the Ideal Parent

Especially at the beginning of a relationship, the pupil may transfer from the Ideal Parent at the level of fantasy or wish fulfilment hoping that: *"This is the teacher who really cares and understands, provides all the warmth, answers all my questions and sees in me great potential".* Such positive and intense feelings can be a source of great inspiration and very motivating for the pupil who then has something wonderful "out there", the vision of his teacher that he can work towards and for. He will *want* to practise to re-evoke and perpetuate the emotions of the lesson, the excitement, appreciation and magic. But the teacher must take care to recognise that such feelings are situation specific: they arise because of the asymmetrical nature of the teacher-pupil relationship and the pupil's transference, and need to be handled with care and respect as such. Only within the safety of the parameters of the professional relationship can the pupil maximise his or her musical potential.

Transference: onto future music lessons and the whole world of music

Whatever the pupil's emotional experience in music lessons, it will be *transferred* onto future music lessons and the wider world of music, determining his desire for or dislike of them.

We need to be aware that, because of the pupil's vulnerability in "Inner Child" and his transference of the role of "Parent" onto the teacher, he will experience any emotion, but particularly negative emotions, with greater intensity. So, for example, if the teacher turns up late, goes to answer the telephone or momentarily switches off, the pupil may feel unduly neglected. Or, if the teacher does not seem to appreciate the effort that the pupil has made, he may feel that she is not only disinterested, but even disapproving. In this way, then, it's easy to understand how straightforward criticism from the teacher can feel like utter annihilation.

It is ironical that, because the teacher's role is dual, both caregiver *and* critic, the pupil looks to the teacher not only to contain his learning anxiety, but also to contain the very anxiety which, as the ultimate authority or critic, she provokes.

Becoming Independent: Strengthening the pupil's "Inner Carer"

Just as the parent brings up the child to be independent, so the teacher's role is to help the pupil become musically independent. As evident from the chapter, in the face of learning anxiety, transference and his own "Inner Critic", the pupil's primary need in becoming independent is to develop his own "Inner Carer", his own inner security and resource. With inner security and resource, he can stay fully present and engaged in learning, even through difficulty, and also feel confident enough to continue learning by himself whether or not he is having lessons.

The "Inner Carer" is developed through positive emotional experience in lessons. In particular, the pupil needs to feel and then internalise acceptance, appreciation and achievement from the teacher.

In practical terms we need to:

- **Give the pupil unconditional positive regard:** The more the pupil experiences unconditional positive regard, belief and trust from the teacher, the more he will internalise and so believe and trust in himself. He needs to feel our belief in him and his potential, whether or not he appears to have talent, because only *then* will he feel safe enough to *try,* because only then will he believe he has a safe place to "fall" (our unerring faith in him) if he gets it wrong. The more he believes and trusts in himself, the more he will *dare* and *discover* within himself.
- **Validate and honour any previous musical achievements:** The pupil will want to show us what he *can* play and has learnt. Our validation of his existing expertise then strengthens his faith in himself, enabling him to feel safe enough to open up to further learning with us.
- **Be constantly in touch with the pupil's feelings:** In particular, we need to be aware of any anxious feelings and be ready to contain them with reassurance, or by giving practical help, or by shifting activity to something the pupil enjoys and can do (See Chapters Two, Four and Five).
- **Give ongoing praise:** Praise is musically life giving. We need to praise whenever it's due and whenever we're in doubt whether it's due. There's always something that can genuinely be felt and said: *"Those two bars were exquisite",* or *"Well done! That was hard, wasn't it?"* Under the considerable time pressure of the lesson it can be only too easy to forget to praise as we tend to feel we must use the time to help the pupil with his difficulties, but this will only give the pupil the message that he'll never be good enough. Perhaps surprisingly, praise can be especially encouraging when there has been little improvement because it can give the pupil the courage to continue to face and conquer his difficulties: *"Oh! So it is worth continuing to try after all!".*
- **Be wary of criticism:** Criticism implies to the pupil that he is not good enough as he is, and is usually felt as a threat. It can be especially devastating if the pupil tried but couldn't succeed. Any constructive comments, so easily felt as criticism, should be preceded by praise: *"I enjoyed that!"* with enough pause for the compliment to sink in, and then put positively: "*You phrased those two notes beautifully! Now apply that from there to there".* Or: *"The legato playing there was lovely. What about bringing out the staccato more to make a real contrast?"*

  In this way the pupil feels secure in our belief in him *now*, so he is then able to hear, accept and take on board what we are saying. If the pupil does not first feel secure, he will put up defences to avoid or lessen the pain: *"It went all right at home!!" "I don't usually do that!" "I'm not listening!"*
- **Know when to criticise:** However, there may be occasions, perhaps in the case of persistent non-practising, despite careful, thorough work in the lesson, when it may be appropriate to deliberately criticise the pupil in order to make him feel more anxious about coming to the lesson-having-not-practised-again than about facing the practice (anxiety blocks learning *unless* it drives!). But this will only work if the teacher-pupil relationship is sufficiently strong and the pupil *can* do what is required, so that he *wants* to work to regain the temporarily lost approval. Otherwise the pupil may feel irredeemably undermined and give up rather than face us with his failure again.

- **Actively encourage a relationship based on reality rather than transference:** We need to actively encourage the pupil to check into what *he* thinks and feels, rather than what he hopes or dreads we think or feel. In this way he learns to trust and rely on himself by taking increasing responsibility for his progress in a spirit of mutual respect, communication and cooperation with us: "Adult" to "Adult" rather than "Child" to "Parent".

Endings

Finally, it is important to be aware that just as beginnings are of particular psychological significance, so are endings. In the same way that the child expects to leave the parental home, so the pupil expects to leave the teacher, not the other way around. If the teacher, for whatever reason, has to leave the pupil, the pupil may experience similar emotions to those of a child whose parents have left him. We must be sensitive about the way we explain our leaving to the pupil, being prepared for him to feel abandoned, betrayed, rejected or angry, and being understanding of his feelings, whatever they may be. Having a cast iron reason for leaving, explaining well in advance and helping the pupil find a new teacher can all help. Unfortunately, in these circumstances, any resentment or anger experienced is often directed at the new, incoming teacher.

Everyone has an Inner Parent, Adult and Child

Inner Parent

Cares and Criticises
Gives love and permission:
"Its ok to be you/do it your way"
Pressurises and drives:
"Be perfect/the best" "You ought to…"

Stress in head when too driven

Inner Adult

Feels good, secure,
Is present, engaged
and responsive to the moment
Resourceful

Head, heart and stomach in alignment

Inner Child

Feels free and is spontaneous
But is easily made anxious,
feeling overwhelmed and unable
Uses defences: Evasion, excuses, emotion

Knots in stomach when anxious

Summary and Practical Checklist

EMOTIONS IN EDUCATION

The Pupil's Emotional Experience and the Role of Teacher

- First impressions are particularly emotionally significant. Make sure the teaching studio is as pleasant and homely as possible, and be warm and welcoming. Especially if the pupil is young, make sure he knows how long he'll be with you, where he should go next or who will collect him, and where the facilities are.
- Anxiety is prevalent: The pupil keys into "Inner Child" having a seemingly out of proportion need for care and fear of criticism. He transfers the role of "Parent", both Caregiver and Critic, onto the teacher.
- The pupil's overriding need is to feel *safe, then* he feels able to learn, as learning involves opening up, trying and taking the risk of failing.
- The pupil picks up messages about himself and his ability to learn through what you feel, do or say. He can then internalise these messages which, if positive, strengthen and, if negative, destroy his inner resource.
- What the pupil hears and internalises, particularly in terms of encouragement or criticism, depends not only on you but also on his innate disposition and previous experiences, internalisations and transferences.
- Notice the pupil's behaviour, especially as he enters. It says much more about him and his transferences than it does about you and your teaching. Whatever his transference he needs to be treated with care, warmth and respect.
- The pupil's experience with you in your studio will, through emotional association, colour his feelings about future lessons and the whole world of music.
- Encourage the pupil to grow into musical independence relying increasingly on his own "Inner Carer" or inner resource. To do this:
- Give unconditional positive regard to the pupil, believing and trusting in him and his potential whether or not he appears to have talent.
- Validate and honour any previous musical experience.
- Always be in touch with his feelings, especially anxious feelings: *"I'll never be able to do this!".* Reassure, "contain" them and give practical help as necessary.
- Praise whenever you feel it is due and whenever you're in doubt whether it's due.
- Teach positively. Begin with praise and then say what needs to be said. For example: *"That chord was very clearly played. Now play this one as clearly".*
- Only use criticism as an incentive to work where the relationship is sufficiently secure.
- Actively encourage a relationship based on reality rather than transference: "Adult" to "Adult" rather than "Child" to "Parent".
- Finally, handle endings with sensitivity, taking care that the pupil does not feel rejected.

Personal Reflection

EMOTIONS IN EDUCATION

The Pupil's Emotional Experience and the Role of Teacher

Reflect briefly on the contents of the chapter. Make a note of the points of particular interest to you below. Then, compile your personal practical checklist on the following page.

Finally, visualise yourself putting any new ideas from your checklist into practice.

Personal Practical Checklist

EMOTIONS IN EDUCATION

The Pupil's Emotional Experience and the Role of Teacher

Chapter Two: Learning and Teaching

Teaching for Learning

"Teaching is the art of communicating knowledge and skills from one person to another. Learning is building up and connecting knowledge and skills with what is already known."

Joseph O'Connor, Not Pulling Strings, 1987

EXERCISE: EXPLORING LEARNING and TEACHING

Answer the questions below, recalling what you did in instrumental or vocal music lessons with the same teachers referred to in Chapter One:

(a) The first teacher you had (at primary school age?)

(b) The second or third teacher you had (at secondary school age?)

(c) A teacher you had aged 18+

Why did you go for lessons?

(a)

(b)

(c)

Who decided what you should learn? You? Your teacher? Or both?

(a)

(b)

(c)

Did you learn everything that what you wanted to learn in terms of pieces, musical styles (classical, pop, jazz etc.) and musical skills (note reading, playing by ear, improvising)? If not, why not?

(a)

(b)

(c)

Were you taught how to work step-by-step, methodically, analysing problems and correcting mistakes (left-brained)? Or were you taught holistically and intuitively, being expected to pick it up through playing from beginning to end (a right-brained approach)?

(a)

(b)

(c)

Did you *practise* step-by-step, methodically, analysing problems and correcting mistakes (left-brained)? Or did you practise holistically, intuitively, playing through from beginning to end to see how it went, picking it up as you went along (right-brained)?

(a)

(b)

(c)

Learning to play a musical instrument requires three main skills:(i) Aural (learning by ear), (ii) Kinaesthetic (learning by physical doing) (iii) Intellectual (learning by understanding and "seeing" shapes and patterns). Arrange these in order (strongest to weakest) according to the way you learnt at each stage:

(a)

(b)

(c)

Now arrange them according to how you practised:

(a)

(b)

(c)

Why did you, and why didn't you practise?

(a)

(b)

(c)

What did your teacher do or what could have been done to help you in practical terms?

(a)

(b)

(c)

Now spend a minute or two considering your answers in terms of understanding how pupils learn and so how we should teach.

Understanding Learning

Pupils learn through emotional engagement: through wanting to, through needing to, through being and remaining open.

They learn holistically, intuitively and unconsciously, *doing* then understanding. And they learn step-by-step, methodically and consciously, *understanding* then doing. From the whole to the parts, the parts to the whole, and back again. They learn through all of their senses and faculties, in particular, in music, through sound, touch and sight, aural, kinaesthetic and intellectual skills, involving emotions, muscles, mind and imagination. They learn through example, demonstration and imitation. They learn through exploration, discovery and creativity. They learn through practising, repeating and remembering.

Through such interaction pupils develop internal representations of skills, concepts and understanding which build up into internal frameworks, each new skill or concept needing to follow directly on from, or be linked with, an existing one. It is the pupil's *internal structure* which constitutes his learning.

Understanding Teaching

The central point for us to remember is that pupils come to lessons in order that they can learn, not so that we can teach. Teaching is *enabling* the pupil to learn: to be open, to interact and to build up his internal structure. The most effective teachers are those who have examined their own learning experiences, analysed their own learning processes and become aware of other possible learning skills. Then they are able to teach *in response* to the pupil, meeting and furthering his interests, and imparting knowledge and skills in the way best suited to his internal processes.

Emotional Engagement: Wanting to learn

Emotional engagement is essential for effective learning. If the pupil is emotionally engaged, both enjoying doing it and feeling able to do it, he will stay connected with it and *try*. If he isn't, he will withdraw, and want to run away.

Perhaps the most important thing for us to do, in this respect, is to ensure that the pupil is learning what he *wants* to learn. We can play a wide variety of music to him to inspire him, and we can try to tune into the vision he has in his mind's eye of what he would like to play. We can ask him what sort of music he would like to play and what musical skills he would like to master, but we need to listen to the replies with wisdom and caution. As pupils are not traditionally consulted about their education, they may think there is a "right" answer to our genuine question, and so misrepresent themselves. Also, they may not know what is on offer and so say they want to do conventional syllabi or grade exams simply because "everyone else does" and, perhaps, their parents encourage this approach. Many teachers too, albeit unconsciously, stick to the standard syllabi, perhaps not knowing what else to teach, or perhaps feeling ill-equipped to teach anything else. Asking the pupil what he wants to learn requires us to be open and courageous: he may want to learn something conventionally considered too hard for him, in which case we'd have to be prepared to teach it unconventionally (see aural, kinaesthetic and intellectual/visual skills below), or he may want to learn something we feel unable to teach, in which case we must feel able to say so and suggest either learning together or putting the pupil in touch with a resource or person who could help. It is usually better to accommodate the pupil's interests, if possible, because much can be learnt and many difficulties surmounted if the pupil really wants to learn.

Holistic (right-brained) and Step-by-Step (left-brained) Skills

The musician needs both left and right-brained skills and uses them simultaneously in both playing and singing.

The right brain is associated with holistic, intuitive, imaginative and subconscious learning, and also with hearing. It perceives and interprets melody and rhythm and operates the left side of the body. The left brain is associated with step-by-step, methodical, intellectual, analytical and conscious learning, and also with seeing. It perceives and interprets language and operates the right side of the body.

Teaching, therefore learning, in *lessons* tends to be step-by-step and methodical: *"First you do this, then you do this".* On the other hand: *"Let's just play it through to see how it goes",* is an intuitive, right-brained approach and characterises much un-thought, but often musical and enjoyable *practice.*

Practising step-by-step and methodically takes considerable intellectual maturity: the pupil needs to be able to interrupt his own musical flow, analyse his own processes and apply the necessary learning skills. It takes patience, it can't be rushed and it can feel unappealing, arid and dry until the pupil learns to connect with the second-by-second perfection of the *process.* Unfortunately, there is no other way to practice for a secure performance. The unconscious, but enjoyable, practice done at home rarely holds water under the slight stress of playing in front of the teacher, let alone the greater stress of public performance: *"It went all right at home!"* being the familiar cry.

Using left-brained skills: step-by-step, methodical, analytical

In order to help the pupil connect with the second-by-second perfection of the process, we need to work step-by-step and methodically with him in lessons, breaking the tasks down into bite-sized pieces, teaching the necessary skills and, above all, playing (at the appropriately slow and secure speed) *with* him. We need to rehearse the tasks and skills with him in lessons until he has securely internalised them. *Then*, through having experienced the benefits of them and by associating them with our warmth and support, he is more likely to practice in that way.

Using right-brained skills: metaphor, imagery and humour

We can alleviate any possible aridity of step-by-step, methodical learning by appealing to the right brain. We can use metaphor, imagery and humour:

Through metaphor and imagery, we can conjure a single picture in our pupils' minds which make a concept or skill immediately graspable. Because the single picture conjured in this way also appeals to the emotions, the concept or skill is made deeply memorable. By being reminded of a metaphor used towards the beginning of Chapter One, this may be more readily appreciated: *"Like animals entering new territory ... ".* Can you remember the meaning this metaphor conveyed and to whom it referred? Perhaps you can even remember the rest of the words? (Click here for more information)

Metaphor and imagery can be particularly useful in conveying musical expression: "Try lightening the staccato to make it sparkle like the sun on the sea", is more evocative than just: "Try lightening the staccato". Likewise: "Make it shimmer like a heat haze over the desert", is more stimulating than: "Make the tremolo softer and more even". Also, images to inspire interpretation can easily be found on the internet, and the pupil may like to search for one or two that feel particularly meaningful and relevant for each of the pieces that he's studying.

Humour and lightness of touch are also very valuable right-brained teaching tools. In seeing the illogical, irrational and absurd, humour can often both ignite creativity and enhance memory. A gently humorous or light touch can also help us manoeuvre more easily in teaching and learning, lessening the chances, or alleviating the reality, of feeling bored, stuck or bogged down. It is a common misconception that "real" work only happens when we are serious.

Aural, Kinaesthetic and Intellectual/Visual Skills

Aural skills (learning by ear), kinaesthetic skills (learning by physical doing) and intellectual/visual skills (learning by understanding and "seeing" shapes and patterns) are all required in learning music, and pupils tend to learn primarily through one or other at different ages. The young beginner is likely to feel happier learning by physical doing, his intellectual understanding then arising out of what he has done. On the other hand, an adult beginner, through years of conventional eye-intellect coordination at school, is more likely to learn first by understanding and then by doing, his finger coordination being slower than his intellectual understanding.

Have you ever considered which of these three skills are most important in music making?

An intellectual imbalance?

In order to make music we only *need* ears and a body: aural and kinaesthetic skills. Indeed, the instinct of most young people whenever they see an instrument (piano, keyboard, percussion etc.) is to go to it and try to make music. But in instrumental lessons, in by far the majority of cases, pupils are first given a book. They are then introduced to the symbols in the book and shown how to use a finger or two to make the corresponding sounds. That done they turn the page, meet another few symbols and use a few more fingers to make those corresponding sounds. So it would seem that, in line with conventional education in which children use intellectual, eye-hand coordination to learn to read and write, conventional music education teaches intellectual, eye-finger coordination to learn to play music(!).

The first problem with eye-finger, rather than ear-finger, learning is that listening and hearing become a secondary rather than primary activity. How often do we have to guide our pupils to listen as well as look and think?

Another problem is that it causes us to feel we must push on to the next page (or the next piece) so long as we have *intellectually*, but not necessarily aurally or kinaesthetically, grasped the current one. One of the results of this is that our pupils rarely have a piece they can play *now,* but are constantly "between" pieces: *"Yes, I learn music, but I can't play anything at the moment. I passed Grade 2 last term, I've forgotten those pieces now, and I am working for Grade 3, but I can't play those pieces yet!"* Another result is performance anxiety as, although we may *think* we have "learnt" the pieces, we are aware they do not *feel* safe. This is because, whether we realise it or not, we have not learnt them at a sufficiently deep kinaesthetic level. To stay in our repertoire, music must be deeply known in both our ears and our muscles.

A further problem is that pupils who learn in this way are very likely to be unable to play without the written music, so they are effectively prevented from expressing themselves spontaneously or from joining in with spontaneous music making. Bringing music and putting it up to play can feel contrived, inappropriate, and set up perfectionist expectations!

But, perhaps worst of all, it is this intellectual/visual bias which is very handicapping to those who are more aurally and kinaesthetically than visually or intellectually able. Such pupils can be put off by the sheer number of intellectual hoops and hurdles that stand between them and the music, however musical they may be.

In view of all of this, and while not devaluing the very valuable and enjoyable skill of being able to read music, we need to balance the required intellectual/visual skills with aural and kinaesthetic skills to enable accessible, secure and deep musicianship for all of our pupils.

Balancing all of the skills

We need to ensure that the pupil is both aware and secure:

Aurally: Does he know the sound he is aiming for?

Kinaesthetically: Does he know what it should feel like? Is he sensitive to what it is feeling like for him as he plays, and is he adjusting to deepen his feelings of physical comfort and security?

Intellectually/Visually: If reading, does he fully understand every symbol on the written page? Can he see and visualise rhythmic shapes, pitch shapes, key shapes and any other significant patterns on the written music *and* on the instrument?

Enjoying strengths and accommodating weaknesses

In order to enjoy strengths and accommodate any weaknesses in the different skills and so maintain the pupil's motivation and musical self-respect, it can be helpful if the teacher works with the three skills at different levels. The following ideas are particularly useful for pupils who are able to play more complex music than they can read, or who can read but want to be able to play by ear or improvise.

Some suggestions to enjoy and develop:

Aural skills

- **The teacher plays to the pupil:** drawing his attention to pulse, rhythm, pitch, phrasing, dynamic, articulation and any other means of musical expression.
- **Singing, then playing by ear:** singing songs to the degrees of the scale can greatly enhance aural awareness and be very helpful for learning to play by ear. So, for example, "Frère Jacques" can first be sung:

  "1 2 3 1, 1 2 3 1, 3 4 5 -, 3 4 5-, etc.", then played.

  Bass lines can also first be sung, then played, in this way. The bass line to "Frère Jacques" is a repeated: "1 5 1 –" and where, as in this case, the bass line consists of chord roots, the pupil could be shown the usual roman numeral chord symbols: "I V I –". Once sung, the bass can either be played as single note roots or full chords depending on the instrument and pupil's ability.

- **Playing by ear:** anything from the simple, well-known tunes that he has sung ("Frère Jacques", Beethoven's "Ode to Joy", Brahms' "Lullaby", Christmas Carols or the current TV jingle) to music which he longs to play but cannot, as yet, easily read.

  Single line tunes could be accompanied by the pupil or the teacher playing single note basses, open fifth and sixth chords or chords I, IV and V etc., as appropriate to the music, pupil and instrument.

  Also, where the tune is difficult to play, perhaps because it ranges over an octave or is syncopated, the pupil can just play the chords to accompany his own or his friends' singing.

- **Improvising:** within clearly set parameters, to enhance the pupil's aural awareness and appreciation of any of the musical elements: pulse and rhythm, pitch and key, scales and melody, chords and chord progressions, phrase patterns and form, style, tone colour, dynamics and articulation. (See Chapter Five).

Kinaesthetic skills

- **The pupil is encouraged to be aware of how it feels to play,** and is shown how to play, adjusting fingers, wrists, elbows, arms, legs, feet and the whole body to maximise physical comfort. Imagining sinking into velvet cushions, kneading dough or deeply massaging the instrument can help as, sensibly, muscles love to learn anything that feels good to them. It is not only harder for the body to learn something that feels physically uncomfortable, but forcing the body against comfort will result in injury. The teacher's understanding of the body and instrument-related technique is essential here.
- **Playing scales, exercises and short sections of pieces:** looking at the fingers and playing slowly, firmly and warmly, concentrating on experiencing the physical sensation as fully as possible.
- **Playing without sound:** on a digital piano with the sound switched off, on the piano lid, without bowing, without blowing to maximise awareness of the physical feel.
- **Hands separately (with and without sound):** so that the left brain (which operates the right-hand side of the body) and right brain (which operates the left-hand side of the body) have a chance to disentangle and become very clear. This can be done on most instruments although on some it will not also be possible to make the intended sound so may be better done only without sound.
- **Hands together:** being aware of which finger (or arm movement) in the left goes with which finger (or arm movement) in the right, remembering that the body feels most comfortable when both left and right are doing the same thing. When left and right are doing different things (different fingers, arm movements, intervals, directions, dynamics etc.) we need more conscious awareness and effort.
- **Using distorted rhythm:** where  becomes , and  becomes , clearly accenting the strong beat(s) of the bar. This helps the body know where to relax (the stronger, longer beats) and where to push through, thus aiding physical comfort and muscle memory, and eliminating the stiffness so often associated with long passage playing.

- **Improvising:** where the pupil plays what he *feels* like playing, physically and emotionally to enhance his physical relationship with the instrument, perhaps within clearly defined parameters (a Twelve Bar Blues) or perhaps on an imaginative theme (A Thunderstorm or The Playground), or perhaps making musical illustrations to poems and stories. (See Chapter Five).

Intellectual/Visual skills

- **Fingering and saying the note names:** without blowing on wind instruments and with and without sound on other instruments. This helps strengthen the mental picture of the notes being played and is a particularly effective way of learning scales and arpeggios and clarifying any tricky passages or more unusual chords in pieces.
- **Note reading:** at an appropriate level for the pupil's ability, ensuring he clearly and thoroughly understands every aspect by breaking the practice down, where necessary, into clearly defined, bite-sized tasks. For example: *"Practice those two bars only: First, count and clap. Second, name the notes as you finger them. Third name the finger numbers as you use them. Finally, sing the counts as you play".*
- **Sight reading:** using music that is both easy and appealing. Perhaps well-known tunes with the titles covered up so the pupil has the fun of identifying the tune from his own playing. Very often pupils are put off sight reading because it feels too hard and the music holds little musical appeal. We could perhaps take a leaf out of conventional education's book where children are sent home with something easy and appealing to read and expected to read it every night, well-known folk tales and fairy stories included. We could have a stock of "library" books to loan out week by week for this.
- **Writing the notes:** that they are learning to read, and then playing them back, or writing down their own improvisation or composition if appropriately simple.
- **Visualising:** "seeing" in the mind's eye, "hearing" in the mind's ear and "feeling" in the mind's muscles to aid learning. This mental rehearsal may *feel* very demanding, requiring both mental concentration and emotional containment of the overriding wish to launch in and play, but the results are powerful, quick and long lasting. Visualisation can be used to clarify anything: notes, fingering, pitch, rhythm, key signatures etc. When a whole piece can be visualised on the instrument, away from the instrument, it will be deeply in memory for even the most demanding performance. As Chopin said: *"Think ten times. Play once".*

Unity and Control

Owing to the variety of different skills required, their different strengths and stages of development, and the ongoing rhythmic propulsion in music, learning to play an instrument is often characterised by a scrabbling, hoping-for-the-best, out-of-control approach.

In order to bring the necessary unity and control to the playing, we need to ensure that the pupil works no faster than the speed at which ears, fingers and intellect can work comfortably and clearly in unison. Playing *with* the pupil at an appropriately slow speed can help ensure this and bolster his confidence and enjoyment.

Perhaps the one single act that, above all, unites left and right brain, aural, kinaesthetic and intellectual skills, is that of singing the counts whilst playing. (Wind players can finger and sing the counts without blowing). If this is done musically, slowly and warmly, giving proper weight to the strong beats in relation to the weak, all of the skills involved are able to unite and sink in at a very deep and secure level: the left (step-by-step, counting, thinking) and right (holistic, pulse, rhythm, pitch) sides of the brain form synapses, uniting in deep rhythm, the body learns exactly where to move and where to relax and the intellect stays clear.

Whole Body Skills

It is also worth mentioning that it is only if the whole self is able to fully experience and internalise the musical elements (pulse, rhythm, pitch, phrasing, mood etc.) that the music can be played from a deeply centred sense of self and therefore be truly expressive. So, especially where pupils are having difficulty with any musical element (pulse, rhythm, pitch, phrasing, expression, quality etc.) it can be helpful to involve the whole body in fully experiencing that element. Then, once internalised through movement, the musical element may be more securely expressed in playing or singing. So, for example, the pupil could:

- step the pulse
- step the rhythm or step the pulse whilst clapping the rhythm
- illustrate the rise and fall of pitch with hand or whole body movement
- illustrate the length of phrase, right through to the end of the last beat, with hand or whole body movement, moving in keeping with the musical quality, and so on.

This approach is dealt with fully in Dalcroze Eurhythmics.

Teaching for Learning

There are two main approaches for learning:

1. **Doing, then understanding**
   Holistic, intuitive, feeling, unconscious ("right-brained")

Associated with hearing

- Listening and expressing
- Using imagination: imagery, metaphor, humour
- Playing by ear, improvising

(Singing, clapping, stepping)

2. **Understanding, then doing**
   Methodical, step-by-step, thinking, conscious ("left-brained")

Associated with seeing

- Looking and understanding
- Using logic: reasoning, analysis, dissection
- Playing by reading notes

(Discussing, reading, writing)

And many subsidiary approaches (using individual senses and faculties):

Aural, Imaginative, Visual, Intellectual, Kinaesthetic, Whole-bodied and Creative

Teaching Styles

The way we teach, of course, depends on the way the pupil is learning. Our teaching style, whether teacher-directed or pupil-directed (or somewhere in between) should be chosen in response to the pupil on the basis of what best serves him, moment to moment, as he builds up his internal structure of skills, concepts and understanding.

Teacher-directed

Traditionally teaching is teacher-directed. The expectation in society and conventional education is that the teacher says what to do, how to do it and a "good" pupil does what he's told.

A teacher-directed style can be the most effective way for the pupil to be given strong feelings of security and to learn particular technical skills from the teacher: *"You do this now, like this ... "*. It can also be particularly inspiring and stimulating for the pupil, opening his eyes to music, knowledge and skills hitherto unknown. However, too much or inappropriate teacher-direction may result in the pupil feeling forced to learn music he doesn't really want to learn and not able to learn what he does want to learn. It may also make him feel under too much pressure to get it right as demanded now. At worst the pupil may feel coerced, angry, rushed, muddled and stupid.

Pupil-directed

A pupil-directed style, where the pupil decides what and how to learn, can be very useful for ensuring the pupil is learning what he wants to learn. By encouraging him to decide his own long and short-term goals, perhaps writing them down in a contract, we may more easily help him keep at it over the inevitable scary or sticky patches, by reminding him of his original vision. Usually pupils have a good feel for their own capabilities and realistically match their abilities with their goals, but where the pupil appears overly ambitious, the teacher can guide him.

Pupil-direction can be the most effective way for the pupil to make connections and discoveries and it can be very helpful for the teacher, now simply observing, to see what the pupil's level of motivation really is, and where any confusion or lack of strategy lies.

Allowing the pupil to work in his own time, and in his own way, can also empower him helping him feel more in control of his own processes (given that he has sufficient learning strategies at his command) and thus keeping any learning anxiety at bay. However, too much pupil-direction may result in the pupil feeling that the teacher has no real interest in his progress, and that he has been left to fend for himself, without sufficient know how and skills. A pupil in this position may feel bored or angry: *"You ought to help, you ought to know, that's what you're here for!* Or he may feel helpless, lost and even abandoned as he keys into infantile emotions.

Both Teacher-directed and Pupil-directed methods have their place:

Most teachers instinctively employ both teacher and pupil direction depending on the needs of the pupil at any given moment. There is undoubtedly a sense in which the teacher "knows best", good teaching being a source of great inspiration for the pupil, successfully analysing the source of difficulty and showing the pupil how to solve difficulties in ways he couldn't easily have worked out for himself. But, the pupil also needs the time and space to make sense of the knowledge or skill he is trying to master, so that it connects with, and is thoroughly assimilated into, his existing understanding and skills.

Much though we might like to we *cannot* spoon feed (teacher-direction), because pupils can only learn by building on their existing frameworks. Very often, where we have shown a pupil what to do but he is finding it difficult, rather than have us persistently trying to get him to succeed, wonders can be worked if we deliberately remove ourselves from the room: *"I'm going to leave you to work that bit out while I go to get a cup of coffee, would you like one?"* Through being freed from the pressure of our presence, the presence of the authority figure, the pupil is more easily able to key into his own processes and so work it out for himself (pupil-direction).

Also, an important part of learning is that the pupil is able to identify exactly what and where the problem is. If he can't yet do this, we can help by asking focusing questions such as:

> *"Where did you feel comfortable and confident?"*
>
> *"So now can you tell me where you would like to feel more comfortable?"*
>
> *"What exactly is it that you need to be able to do there?"*

Then, when he has identified what he wants, he can actively seek our help, rather than passively accepting it, or letting it blow over the top of his head! He can come to us with specific questions or problems (pupil-direction), and our teaching can turn on the necessary, and most welcome, light bulb (teacher-direction).

There are two main teaching styles:

1. Teacher-directed
The pupil does what the teacher says

- Can reduce anxiety - the pupil knows what's expected
- Often the most effective way for the pupil to learn new knowledge and skills
- But the pupil can feel forced down a route of little interest, at the wrong pace

2. Pupil-directed
The teacher follows the pupil's lead, letting him decide what, when and how to learn

- Can reduce anxiety - the pupil knows he won't be criticised
- Often the most effective way to ensure the pupil is learning what he wants to learn, and at the right pace
- But the pupil can feel lost, not knowing what to do, or how to do it.

Both styles are useful, depending on the pupil's moment to moment needs.

Role reversal

Having the pupil "teach" us can be one of the most effective teaching tools of all. As we know, teaching a concept or skill both requires and results in a deeper understanding and internalisation of the concept or skill, and many pupils enjoy "testing" the teacher on whatever they themselves have learnt. If done in an appropriately light and appreciative spirit, it can be both helpful and fun.

The Key is in Success

Above all, the key for each pupil is in "being able to do it", in success. The more the pupil can play, the more he will want to play. They practise when they *can* play it, don't they?!

Through good teaching in the lesson and the internalisation of effective learning strategies, the pupil gradually becomes able both to identify what is required and to *feel* able and *be* able to do it, so becoming musically independent.

Summary and Practical Checklist

LEARNING AND TEACHING

Teaching for Learning

- The pupil comes to lessons so he can learn (not so that we can teach).
- He learns through *interaction* with the material using all of his senses and faculties. In this way he builds up his own *internal* structure of concepts and skills, each new concept or skill having to being connected with or linked into his pre-existing internal structure.
- He learns through emotional engagement, so inspire him by introducing him to wonderful music and ask him what he would like to learn. If he wants to learn something conventionally considered too hard, be prepared to teach unconventionally.
- Notice the pupil's preferred methods of learning: Intuitive (right-brained)? Step-by-step (left-brained)? and match teaching appropriately so that he can enjoy his strengths and strengthen his weaknesses.
- "Contain" or "frame" tasks into bite-sized pieces so the task feels clear and manageable, rather than vague and overwhelming.
- Have the pupil learn new skills thoroughly in the lesson because he practises when he *can* do it and when he's confident of results.
- Use intuition, metaphor and imagery to inspire and bring deep memory to learning.
- Whatever is being studied, encourage the pupil to use Aural, Kinaesthetic and Intellectual/Visual skills so that he knows what every note *sounds* like (aural), *feels* like (kinaesthetic) and *looks* like (visual/intellectual).
- Encourage the use of different skills so that he can both enjoy his strengths and strengthen his weaknesses at appropriately different levels: by ear, improvising or note reading.
- Encourage the pupil, perhaps by playing with him, to play, with warmth, at the speed at which ears, fingers and intellect can comfortably unite in clarity.
- Make singing the counts while playing (or while fingering, without blowing, on wind instruments) a priority. Singing the counts, above all, helps unity and control of all the skills required.
- Be ready to use both teacher-direction *("Try this, like this")* and pupil-direction *("What would you like to learn? How are you going to learn it?")* as best suits the pupil from moment to moment. Useful phrases in pupil-directed learning:

  "What would you like to work on next?"

  "Can you identify exactly what the problem is there? (Notes? Rhythm? Fingering?)"

  "Where did you feel comfortable and confident? ... Where would you like to feel more comfortable and confident?"

  "I've never tried! Let's try together."

  "I don't know, but I'll find out for you."
- Make success, that is: "being able to do it" a priority.

Personal Reflection

LEARNING AND TEACHING

Teaching for Learning

Reflect briefly on the contents of the chapter. Make a note of the points of particular interest to you below. Then, compile your personal practical checklist using the following page.

Finally, visualise yourself putting any new ideas from your checklist into practice.

Personal Practical Checklist

LEARNING AND TEACHING

Teaching for Learning

Chapter Three: Emotions, Motivation and Practice

"Images received from the unconscious can give you important information about yourself and advise on the most suitable course of action.

With the power of your imagination, ...with practice, as your actions follow suit, ...you will be able to achieve your goals."

Rachel Charles, Your Mind's Eye, 2000

EXERCISE: EXPLORING EMOTIONS AND MOTIVATION

Think of something, whether professional or domestic, that you know you ought to do but that you keep putting off (the tax return form? The awkward letter? The re-decorating? Or that enormous pile of ironing?).

When you have settled on one thing, allow it to come into your mind and be aware of the imagery of it in your mind. What is it like? (Dense and dark? Awkward and spikey? Or, perhaps, so high you can't see over the top?)

Now draw your image of it:

Find one word or a short phrase which expresses your feelings about the task you are putting off:

The following drawing depicts a teacher's imagery about the essay she has been putting off, but which she has to write in order to complete her coursework to gain the further professional qualification she wants:

Word processor

Dark Oppression

The words the teacher chose were: *"Black and oppressed"*. Other words that come up regularly in doing this exercise are:

> *Frustrated, stressed, pressurised, guilty, overwhelmed, anxious, panicked, frightened, put off, reluctant, resentful, besieged, trapped, seething, dark, depressed, despairing, powerless, helpless, stuck, confused, muddled, doubtful, vague, cluttered, chaotic, disorganised, disinterested, bored, tired.*

Read through the above words again allowing yourself to *feel* them.

That is how our pupils feel about their practice if they are not practising.

Next, imagine this task completed as you would like it to be and then draw an image of the completion. (At this stage it may become clear to you that you don't wish and have no need to do this task. If so, think *why*, and then pick something else and start the exercise again):

Find a word or short phrase which expresses your feelings about your completed task:

Below is the teacher's image of completion:

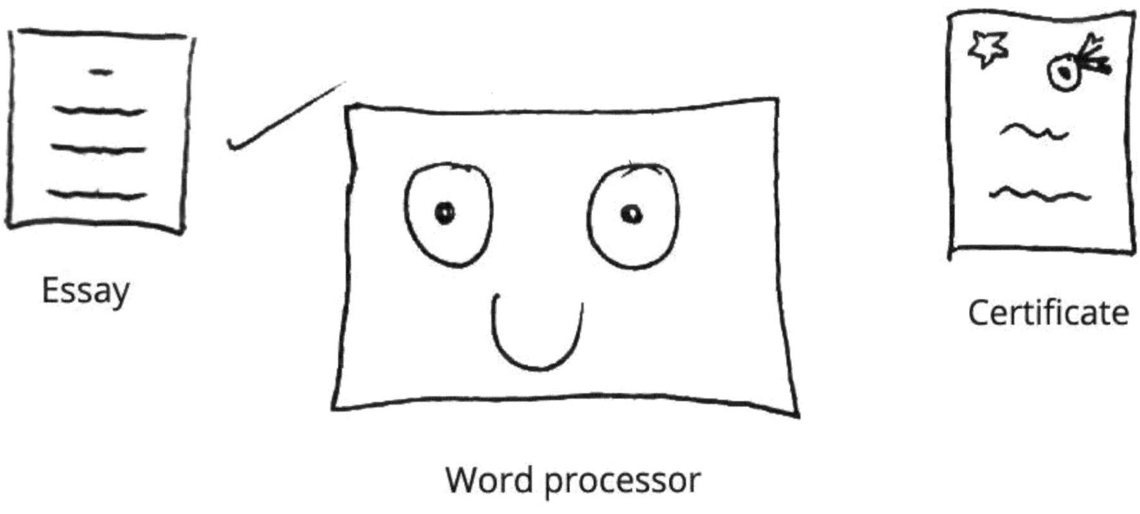

The teacher's words were: *"Clear and relieved"*.

Other descriptions commonly arising at workshops are:

> *Bright, light, clear-sighted, orderly, under control, uncluttered, competent, focused, organised, integrated, hopeful, made progress, achieved, relieved, content, happy, joyful, uplifted, fulfilled, confident, strong, on top, excited, radiant, amazed, big, proud, rewarded, creative, omnipotent, calm, relaxed, peaceful, serene.*

Now how do you now feel about tackling your put-off task? Why?

The chances are that you will feel more like doing it, because you now have a clearer mental picture of the goal. So long as the goal is what you want, the clear mental picture will have strengthened your emotional connection with it and tugged you closer.

If you *don't* now feel more like doing it, it may be because the *process* of doing of it holds no appeal.

So, now think about your *process,* and, if necessary, think how to make the process more *appealing.* Then sum up your plan in a phrase or two:

The given teacher's phrase was: *"Allocate time and get on with it".*

Other phrases that regularly come up are:

> *Prioritise, sort and decide, make a decision, make a plan, structure time, create space, put it in the diary, get up very early for a few days, organise, create a realistic timetable, decide the method, build up confidence, seek advice, get professional help, stick at it.*

Ways of making it more appealing include:

> *Focusing on one thing at a time, doing the hard bits first, leaving the nice bits until last, breaking the task down into small steps and rewarding each step. Spending an allocated number of minutes each day and then leaving it (whether or not there's been progress). Promising myself a reward (with a cup of coffee, a tic tac, boiled sweet or biscuit, putting money into a kitty to treat myself), making the working area as pleasant as possible (music, flowers, candles), getting a friend involved.*

Now spend a minute or two considering the implications of this exercise in terms of understanding pupils' motivation, and motivating them to practise.

Understanding Motivation

It is the *feeling* that the pupil experiences when he contemplates practice which causes him to move towards or away from practice. He is likely to move towards practice which holds the promise of lightness, brightness and success, and move away from practice which threatens fog, darkness and difficulty. In order to be persuaded to practise through difficulty, he must be able to feel or "see" in his mind's eye the light, bright success beckoning at the end. He also needs to be able to feel or "see" *how* he's going to do it, and the more pleasant and manageable this is, the more he will feel motivated to do it. It helps, too, if he can "see" *why, when and where* to do it.

Accessing Pupils' Feelings

In the light of this, the more we can access how the pupil feels about his practice the better, and we may need to help him transform his feelings. We can find out how the pupil is feeling through observing him and through asking him. But, particularly in our society in which the acknowledgement of feelings is not traditionally encouraged, he may or may not show his feelings, and he may or may not tell us. He may not even be aware of his own feelings, in which case he *can't* tell us or he may feel he "ought not" to feel those negative feelings, in which case he *won't* tell us. In order to tell us at all, the pupil needs to feel assured that he is safe and won't be either ridiculed or reprimanded, and for this it can be helpful to work with him through imagery:

Accessing pupils' feelings through imagery

Accessing the pupil's feelings about practice through imagery enables both the pupil and the teacher to become aware of any hitherto unconscious feeling. From being nameless and nebulous in semi-consciousness, feelings about practice can become evident, and contained on a piece of paper, so that they can be faced, thought about and then acted on rationally.

To work with imagery:

- Ask the pupil to let the thought of practice come to him and to be aware of the feeling or imagery surrounding the thought.
- Ask him to draw the image, or describe it so that you can draw it. (Technical ability to draw is unimportant. The point is to allow your feelings to express themselves through your pencil so that you can then see what they *look* like.)
- Ask him what he would like to do about it. Remember always to ask "open" questions, empathetically, to elicit his feelings without bias or influence from you (For more about "open questions" see Chapter Four).
- Keep the work with imagery "real", that is, within the bounds of physical possibility.
- Translate the imagery back into practicality by asking what it represents and so defining what the pupil is going to do.

An example of using imagery with a fifteen-year-old pupil who was avoiding practice:

Teacher: *"Imagine yourself at home. The thought comes to your mind that you should practice your Grieg (the specific piece he was avoiding practising). What sort of image comes to your mind with the thought of practice?"*

Pupil: *"It's like a block."*

Teacher: *"What sort of a block?"* asking an "open" question being careful not to influence the pupil's imagery.

Pupil: *"Like a wall".*

Teacher: *"A wall"* repeating gently so the pupil feels heard, and continuing:

"How high is the wall?" another "open" question.

Pupil: *"Taller than me".*

Teacher: *"Would you like to draw it or would you like me to?"*

Pupil: *"You".*

Teacher: *"Like this?"* drawing a line nearly at the top of the page to indicate the height of the wall.

Pupil: *"Yes!"*

Teacher: *"What's it made from?"*

Pupil: *"Red brick".*

Teacher: *"Like this?"* sketching it in.

Pupil: *"Yes".*

Teacher: Pauses to let it all sink in. Then:

"What do you want to do?"

Pupil: *"I want to get over it."*

Teacher: *"Okay. How are you going to do that?"*

Pupil: *"I'll jump!"*

Teacher: Empathetically and warmly: *"You can't, can you? It's higher than you."*

It is important to keep within the bounds of physical possibility in working with the imagery because the original imagery (in this case, the red brick wall and the pupil's size in relation to it) accurately reflects the amount of difficulty the pupil felt in relation to the task.

Pupil: *"Okay, I'll climb it then".*

Teacher: *"How? There aren't any handholds or footholds in red brick are there?"* always empathetically, warmly.

Pupil: Thinks, and then: *"Well, you haven't seen this, but there are some crates over there off the right hand side of the picture. I'm going to carry them over, one or two at a time, and pile them up so I can climb over the wall".*

Teacher: *"Ah! Like this?"* drawing crates along the bottom of the wall and piling them up layer by layer.

Pupil: Maintains enormous emotional connection and it doesn't take long to realise that five crates are needed on the bottom layer, then a layer of four, then three, then two, then one to get to the top and over.

After a moment or two of mutual satisfaction:

Teacher: *"So what do the crates represent for you?"* This is important in order to translate the solution back into practical use

Pupil: *"Oh! The difficult bars, the difficult chords! I see! I just have to tackle it crate by crate, I don't have to face the whole thing at once, just bit by bit and I'll get there!"*

Through the exercise, the pupil was enabled to discover his own feelings of block *("a wall"),* his own feelings of what he wanted to do about it *("I want to get over it")* and his own way of getting over it *("bit by bit").* Although the teacher was sure the pupil loved the music and wanted to study it at the outset, *and they had practised it "bit by bit" in the lesson*(!), no progress was made until the pupil had become conscious of his hitherto nameless, nebulous, negative feeling, worked with it through imagery, and found out what to do and how to do it for himself.

Accessing pupils' feelings using self-report practice sheets

Self-report practice sheets, in which the pupil has to write what was enjoyed and what was avoided in practice, and why, can also be very useful in helping the pupil become aware of his own motivational forces. Many pupils may prefer to access their feelings in this way, in the privacy of their own practice, rather than in front of the teacher. The sheets also provide a means of accountability: having to fill in the sheet helps ensure some practice is done.

An example is given below:

Self-Report Practice Sheet

NAME:

DATE:

Please record the number of minutes/hours spent practising:

DAY 1

DAY 2

DAY 3

DAY 4

DAY 5

DAY 6

I particularly enjoyed practising:

DAY 1

DAY 2

DAY 3

DAY 4

DAY 5

DAY 6

Reasons for practising:

DAY 1

DAY 2

DAY 3

DAY 4

DAY 5

DAY 6

I avoided practising (please refer to the manuscript book to see what should have been practised):

DAY 1

DAY 2

DAY 3

DAY 4

DAY 5

DAY 6

Reasons for not practising or avoiding practising certain things:

DAY 1

DAY 2

DAY 3

DAY 4

DAY 5

DAY 6

Additional Notes:

Common Feelings Underlying Lack of Practice

The more usual feelings behind lack of practice stem from not wanting to do it, not knowing what to do, not knowing how, why, when or where to do it and could be expressed as follows:

- *"Seeing myself doing it in my mind's eye holds no personal satisfaction, no kudos, no street cred, no fun: I don't* ***want*** *to do it".*
- *"My mind's eye doesn't come up with what I ought to practise and it seems too much of an effort to look in the practice note book: I don't know* ***what*** *to do".*
- *"Just thinking about it gives me negative feelings. It seems foggy, dark and difficult: I don't know* ***how*** *to do it".*
- *"I don't feel intrinsic reward and there is no extrinsic incentive or goal. My teacher doesn't mind whether I do it or not!: I don't know* ***why*** *to practice, it doesn't matter".*
- *"There is not time and space in my mind's eye to do it. My (or my family's) life style is too cluttered and disorganised: I don't know* ***when or where*** *to practice"*

Practical Suggestions to Motivate Pupils to Practise

Wanting to practise

The pupil is more likely to want to practise if *he* sets his own practice in line with his own positive feeling, interests and abilities, in discussion with the teacher. He may like to do this lesson by lesson, or he may like to go one step further, setting his own long and short-term goals, perhaps in the form of a contract, with the teacher. In this way he is likely to feel both more responsible and more accountable, and so practise more.

Knowing WHAT to practise

The more the pupil knows and can see in his mind's eye what to practise, the more he is likely to go and do it. To help him know and see, we could ask him to tell us at the end of the lesson, and we could ask him to write it down. It may well take longer for him to write, but writing is a good means of remembering. Also, if we ask him to write something informative such as: *"Practise A Minor, the relative minor to C Major"* he can be learning at the same time. Finally, if he does forget and needs to look it up, it will be in his own familiar, and therefore more inviting, writing.

Knowing HOW and *feeling* able

As discussed in Chapter One, learning anxiety, that is, the fear of "not being able to do it", is almost inevitable. In order to *feel* like practising, the pupil must *feel able* to do it, *or* feel enough inner resource to be able to sit with the "not knowing" and try. One of the ways we can strengthen the pupil's inner resource is by ensuring that everything the pupil tackles in the lesson is accompanied by warm and successful feelings so that the emotional association entices him towards, rather than puts him off practice. We can also say things during lessons which, if he internalises, would be helpful for him to say to himself as he practises, for example:

"Let's start with something you enjoy!"

"What would you like to do next?"

"Now let's have a go at this (hard) bit. We'll start by taking it from there to there."

"Well done! That was hard and you stuck it out!"

"Time to stop now. Look what you've achieved today!"

Knowing HOW and *being* able

The pupil also needs to know how and *be* able to do it. *Feeling* able will enable him to try and then *be* able. *Being* able usually makes him *feel* able but not always. Sometimes he can *be* able but still not *feel* able which is why he still won't practice even though we know he's done it successfully in the lesson.

For the pupil to *be* able *and* feel able it is important that we teach the necessary practical skills in the lesson and rehearse them with the pupil in the lesson until he has internalised them. In this way he will gradually feel confident and familiar enough with them to use them in the privacy of his own practice.

Teaching the necessary practical skills usually involves "containing" or "framing" tasks into manageable bite-sized portions and employing appropriate learning strategies (see Chapter Two). Some examples are:

"Count and clap the rhythm from the first beat of that bar to the first beat of the next bar".

"Set the kitchen timer for 5 minutes, then "finger and say" D major descending".

"Use distorted rhythm to practice that fast moving passage"

"Think first. Wait until you have a clear mental picture of exactly which finger plays which note when, then play".

In order to try to ensure that the pupil *is* able and *feels* able to do it at home, we can ask him to explain and demonstrate to us what he is going to do.

Knowing WHY: Reasons for practising

The pupil is more likely to practise if he feels:

Intrinsic Reward: *Enjoying it now,* having positive emotional association and connection with practice.

External Incentives: Dates to play to fellow pupils, family, friends, examiners and a public audience. These special dates need not only be performances of pieces, they can be of scales, sight-reading, improvisation or composition as follows:

Scale concerts can be very effective especially if scales are played in such a way that music is made. For example, some pupils could play the scale in semibreves, some in minims and some in crotchets simultaneously, or perhaps each pupil could begin two or four notes after the previous one.

Sightreading get togethers (or informal concerts) can be presented as quiz evenings with pupils having to sight read well known tunes for themselves or the audience to identify (teachers remembering to have covered up the titles first!)

Improvisation, particularly as a group activity, can also be inspiring and relaxing. For ideas, see Chapter Five.

Extrinsic Reward: Stars, stickers, sweets, pennies, a collection fund for an end of term visit to the music shop and home-made certificates (easy to produce on word processing programmes) can all be incentives to practice.

Many pupils respond to deciding on their own reward system. They are often the best judges of how much reward is appropriate, knowing truly how much work was put in. Where a pupil does want to decide his own reward, the teacher's job is usually to make sure the pupil is being sufficiently encouraging and rewarding.

The Teacher's Appreciation: The thought of the teacher's radiant and appreciative smile can keep the pupil practising all week, or, at least, more than he otherwise would! So it is important that we make sure we notice and appreciate any progress. Also, appreciation can be particularly encouraging when there has been little progress as it can help the pupil feel that it is worth continuing to try after all.

Keeping clear records of work done in the lesson can help us be aware of progress made from week to week.

Accountability: In by far the majority of cases, pupils only work at that for which they know they'll be held accountable. (Why do they do their homework? Because it has to be handed in on time and there are sanctions if it's not!) For this it can help if the teacher keeps an *independent* record of the goals set and agreed at the last lesson so she always has concrete evidence to refer to in holding the pupil accountable as pupils often "forget" their practice note book when they don't want us to remember what's in it!. A register style book from the stationers can be very useful for this.

Other ways of holding pupils accountable include:

Self-Report Practice Sheets: in which the pupil writes down what he practised when (perhaps including *reasons* for avoiding practising anything, see the example given earlier in the chapter). The very fact that the sheet has to be filled in ensures some practice is done.

Requiring the pupil to record parts of his practice: and email or bring the recording to the lesson for the teacher to listen to during the week. It need not be listened to all through but just "spot checked" when convenient (perhaps when in the car?).

Having a contract with parents and requiring a parental signature in the practice notebook.

Fear of the consequences of not practising: A healthy fear can drive the pupil to practise: he can have a healthy fear of letting himself down in front of the group, school, examiner or teacher and so practice to avoid this. He can have a healthy fear of the teacher's disapproval or criticism and so practice to avoid that. However, we must be careful how we express disapproval or criticism: it only works in a warm and secure relationship and when the pupil feels that he *can* succeed and wants to fight (practise) to regain the temporarily lost approval, otherwise he will feel severely threatened, unable to live up to our expectations and want to run away.

Knowing WHEN and WHERE: Time and space to practise

Most pupils, especially young ones, like to have a space to practise which is, as far as possible, at the hub of family life, perhaps in a living room or hall where the instrument is kept ready and the music left invitingly open. In this way the odd five minutes is done *en passant* because the pupil *feels* like it *now*.

Again, most pupils, especially young ones, are more likely to practise when an encouraging parent (or other empathetic adult) is close by, making encouraging and appreciative (only!) comments, perhaps while otherwise occupied. (One pupil's practice dramatically increased when his mother set up the ironing board near the piano. The sheets were much improved too!)

Older pupils may like parents to stay well out of the way while they're practising, but the odd appreciative comment from parents: *"That was sounding lovely!"* can do much to encourage playing.

Even adult pupils may need help in organising time for practice, perhaps being encouraged to write their practice times in their diaries. They may also need help in understanding and handling their own reluctance to tackle difficulties. Discussing what, how, why, when and where with the teacher can be very helpful and motivating for them.

Pupils practise when they:

- Can see ***what*** to do, and ***where*** and ***when*** to do it, clearly, in their mind's eye
- Know ***how*** to do it, having done it, or something similar, before
- Have a ***reason*** to do it - goal or deadline
- Are ***confident*** of progress and success

Are organised - feel able - need - can succeed

When Pupils *Still* Don't Practice

However, we also need to be aware that there will always be some pupils who are simply not going to practise, whatever we do, for a variety of psychological and social reasons (see Chapter Four for more on understanding negative energy in pupils). We are always free to choose whether to continue to teach such a pupil. But, so long as the pupil wants to come to lessons, it is usually better both for him personally and for his musical development if we don't give up on him as this may simply confirm him in his belief that no one cares and that he's no good. Instead, we could simply accept him and the situation as it is, and focus on enjoying making music together in the lesson. Sometimes the desire to practise follows, but sometimes not until *years* later, and sometimes not at all.

EMOTIONS, MOTIVATION AND PRACTICE

- Feelings cause pupils to move towards or away from practice.
- Pupils practise when they can feel or "see" in their mind's eye lightness, brightness and success about their practice.
- They don't practise when they feel or "see" darkness, fog or difficulty.
- Pupils need to feel or "see" the lightness, brightness and success beckoning to them at the end before they can be persuaded to set out and find a way through difficulty.

We need to:

- Be aware of the pupil's feeling behind his practice, particularly if he is not practising. Find this out through talking with the pupil, or, perhaps more reliably, through working with imagery or through using a self report practice sheet.

The pupil needs (or may like) to:

- Feel intrinsic motivation: *wanting* to practise, having positive emotional association and connection with practice.
- Feel in charge, setting his own long and short-term goals and deciding on his own rewards.
- Have a clear picture of what to practise in his mind's eye (rather than in the practice note book). Asking him to tell us what, how, why, when and where will help make his mind's eye images clearer.
- Feel able to do it. Have enough emotional inner resource to be able to "sit with not knowing" while patiently working it out.
- Be able to do it. Have enough practical resource to be able to "contain" and "frame" tasks and employ appropriate strategies.
- Have external incentives: playing to fellow pupils or friends in concerts, festivals or exams, not only pieces and ensembles but also scales, sight-reading, improvisation and composition.
- Have extrinsic rewards: perhaps stars, stickers, sweets, a fund for the music shop etc.
- Feel praised and encouraged, having genuinely pleased teachers, parents and examiners.
- Be held accountable: The teacher needs to keep clear, independent records of the practice set making the pupil answerable to anything not achieved. The pupil could also be asked to fill in a practice sheet, record his practice on cassette and have his parents put their signature to the amount of time spent practising.
- Fear the repercussions if he *doesn't* practise, both fearing what the teacher may say and fearing letting himself down. Fear can be an effective driver so long as the pupil feels sufficiently secure in himself, his practice and his teacher.
- Be clear, perhaps with parents' help or through discussion with the teacher, when and where to practise.

Personal Reflection

EMOTIONS, MOTIVATION AND PRACTICE

Reflect briefly on the contents of the chapter. Make a note of the points of particular interest to you below. Then, compile your personal practical checklist on the following page.

Finally, visualise yourself putting any new ideas from your checklist into practice.

Personal Practical Checklist

EMOTIONS, MOTIVATION AND PRACTICE

Chapter Four: Maintaining Positive Energy

Dealing with Negative Feeling

"We should wisely remember that we are our own most important counselling instrument and what we know and possess of ourselves makes a great difference in whether we help others effectively or not."

Eugene Kennedy and Sara C. Charles,

On Becoming a Counsellor, 1977

EXERCISE: EXPLORING ENERGY

Bring to mind a pupil (Pupil "A") whom you very much enjoy teaching. Allow an image of a lesson with this pupil to come to you. Draw the image below.

Lesson with Pupil A:

Example of a lesson with a typical Pupil A:

Find a word or short phrase to express the feelings that are embodied in the image:

Examples:

Fully present and engaged, focused, spontaneous, energetic, exciting, easy, light, fun, warm, caring, nurturing, trusting, communicating, honest, safe, loving, flowing, challenging, joyful, inspiring, sparkling, magic.

Write down your thoughts as you teach this pupil:

Examples:

"This is fun"; "Isn't he amazing?"; "What's the best way of tackling this is? Ah yes!". The realisation that when "in flow" nothing awkward or disturbing, enters thoughts or feelings.

Was the energy flowing from the teacher? The pupil? Neither? Or both?

Understanding Positive Energy

In the given example above it is clear that there is a mutual flow of positive energy from both teacher and pupil, in psychological terms: "Adult" to "Adult". Such energy arises where both teacher and pupil are readily and happily engaged in the work, both feel security and trust in themselves, their ability and each other, and both feel free to take the initiative and to respond to the other's initiative. In such a situation there's a sense that anything can happen, everything is new in the moment and it's exciting and alive. We find ourselves teaching something we didn't know we knew, or saying something in a way which sheds new light even for us. It is, literally, creation in action.

A typical good lesson

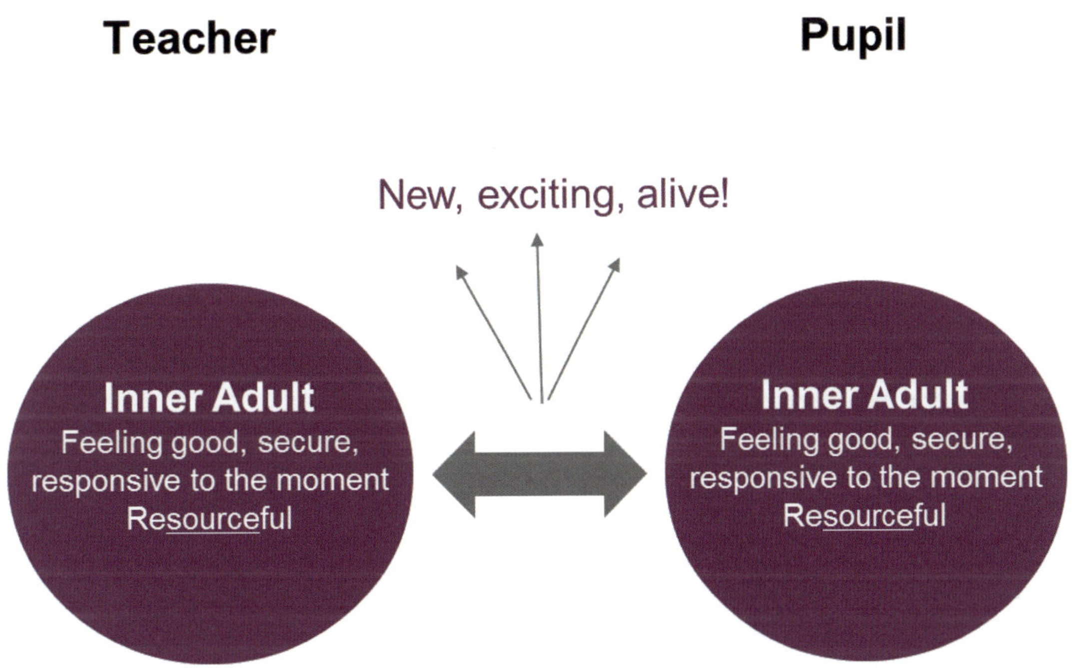

Both teacher and pupil are comfortably engaged. There is a two-way flow of energy through which ideas and insights emerge, making the lesson feel new in the moment, exciting and alive.

Now bring to mind two differing pupils (Pupils B (i) and B (ii)) with whom you are not as happy as you would like to be, and go through the same procedure:

Allow an image of a lesson with your selected Pupil B (i) to come to you. Could you draw the image?

Pupil B (i):

Find a word or short phrase to express the feelings that are embodied in the image:

Write down your thoughts as you teach this pupil:

Was energy flowing from the teacher? The pupil? Neither? Or both?

Now allow an image of a lesson with your selected Pupil B (ii) to come to you. Could you draw the image?

Pupil B (ii):

Find a word or short phrase to express the feelings that are embodied in the image:

Write down your thoughts as you teach this pupil:

Was energy flowing from the teacher? The pupil? Neither? Or both?

Example of a Pupil B:

The imagery:

Words or short phrases that describe the feeling:

Resentful, angry, pressured, stressed, frustrated, blocked, brick-walled, exhausted, like a dead weight.

Thoughts that went through the teacher's mind:

> *"We must get on."*
>
> *"It'll never be ready in time."*
>
> *"What will the parents think?"*
>
> *"If the examiners ... or audience ... hears it like this they'll think I'm a useless teacher!"*
>
> *"He ought to do these scales and exercises."*
>
> *"He ought not to play by ear."*
>
> *"Help! I can't teach jazz improvisation! So we won't do it!"*
>
> *"Why can't he just practise as I showed him? Then he'd be able to do it!"*

It can be seen that all of the energy is coming from the teacher. The teacher is trying very hard. The pupil is not interacting.

A typical difficult lesson

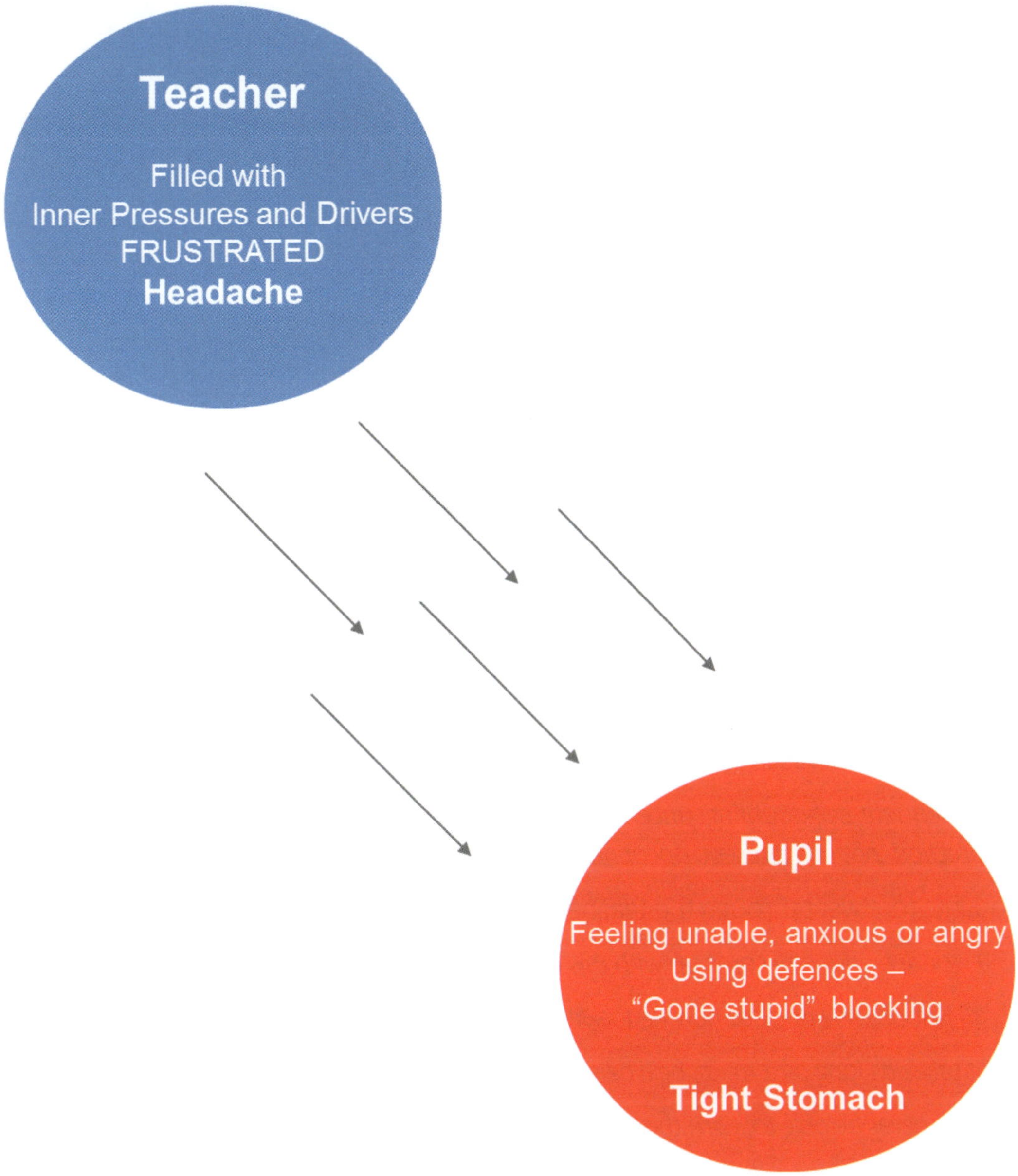

The teacher is (unconsciously) in ***Critical Parent*** and the pupil is in ***Inner Child.*** The harder the teacher tries, the worse the pupil feels.

Example of another Pupil B:

The imagery:

Words or short phrases to describe the feeling:

Inadequate, self-doubting, uncertain, confused, bored, disinterested, helpless, unfocused, lost direction, not fully present, unconnected.

Thoughts that went through the teacher's mind:

"I wonder what he'll come up with this week!"

"I'll just observe and see how he tackles it."

"It takes as long as it takes; he'll be ready when he's ready."

"He'll never be able to learn this ... I'll never be able to teach it to him."

"He hasn't practised again. I'm not going to bother myself."

"It's his responsibility, it's up to him."

"When's break?"

"zzzzzzzzzzzzzzzzzzzzzzzzzzzzzzzzzzzzzzzzzzzz"!

In this case, there is no energy either from teacher to pupil, or from pupil to teacher.

Another typical difficult lesson

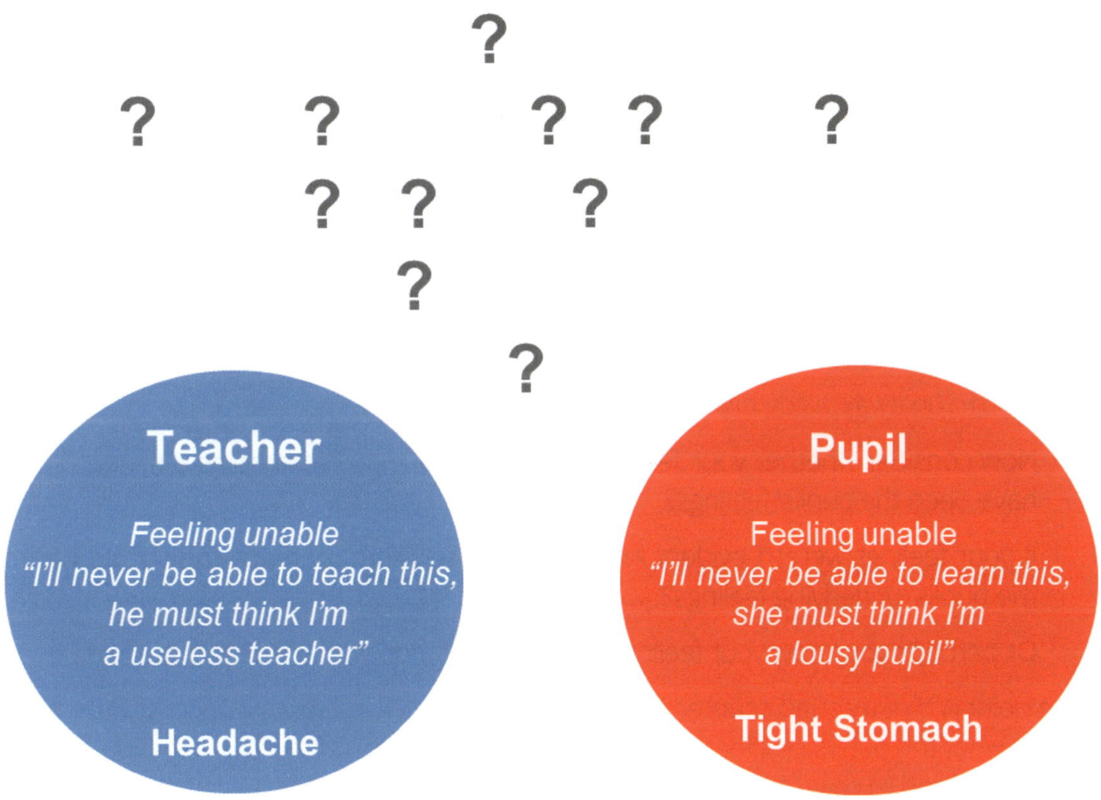

Both teacher and pupil have keyed into ***Inner Child***
feeling anxious and helpless.
(This is usually "countertransference"…)

Being Aware of Energy

It's the teacher's and pupil's *feelings* in the lesson (which can be accessed through imagery) which determine the quality of energy in the lesson. So we need to be aware of both our pupil's and our own feelings, and we need to be able to understand and handle those feelings to make the most of positive energy.

Using Countertransference

We can know our pupil's feelings through our *own* feeling. Our own feeling in lessons, whether of excitement, appreciation, magic, or lack of confidence, frustration and antipathy, may actually be telling us what the pupil is feeling, as feelings travel gut to gut, by-passing reason. This communication of feeling is called *countertransference* and is widely used as a psychotherapeutic tool in enabling therapists, through their own feeling, be aware of the client's feeling. So, as we experience our own feelings, we need to consider whether they are the pupil's feelings.

In the given example of the first Pupil B, for instance, the teacher was aware that she was feeling: *"Resentful, angry, pressured, stressed, frustrated, blocked, brick-walled, exhausted, like a dead weight".* So was the pupil feeling the same? He could have felt *all* of these feelings if he was feeling forced down a route he didn't wish to take, at a speed or in a way that felt too difficult for him and if he was then defending himself, albeit unconsciously, by resisting and refusing to cooperate.

In the given example of the second Pupil B, the teacher was feeling: "Inadequate, self-doubting, uncertain, confused, bored, disinterested, helpless, unfocused, lost direction, not fully present, unconnected". Again, was the pupil feeling the same? He could have if he felt very inadequate about his own ability, having no idea where to start or what to do, believing that, as the teacher wasn't helping, she felt he was useless and not worth taking the time with, all of which would make him run away inside himself, longing for it all to be over.

> Now consider whether your feelings in lessons with your examples B (i) and B (ii) could have been the pupils' feelings?
>
> If your feelings weren't evident in the pupils' behaviour, perhaps they could have been the pupils' underlying feelings?
>
> Or perhaps you know your feelings had nothing to do with the pupils' feelings?

The point is that through countertransference, or our own feeling, we at least have a hypothesis about what the pupil's real feelings are. This is particularly useful in our stiff upper lip society where we tend to cover feelings up: an anxious pupil may hide his anxiety through fear of being considered a failure, or *"uncool",* and a bored pupil may hide his disinterest and dislike through good manners. But if *we* are feeling anxious, or bored, then we need to consider the possibility that the pupil is too, whether or not he is showing it. It sounds simple, and in a way it is, but recognising and dealing with negative feeling is not always straightforward.

Difficulties in Recognising Pupils' Negative Feelings

Whereas positive feelings fill us with inner security, making it easy for us to be open to the pupil and he to us, negative feelings are disabling. Wherever they come from, feelings of inferiority, inadequacy and uselessness can cause us to withdraw into ourselves, and feelings of frustration or anger can cause us to lose hold of ourselves. So, it can be very hard for us to dare to consider whether, much less believe that, our own negative feelings are telling us what the pupil is feeling.

Also, if our negative feelings make sense in the given situation, it can be harder still. For example, if a young teacher teaching a smartly-suited businessman twice her age felt inferior during lessons, she may easily assume that *he* was finding *her* teaching disappointing. But it could have been *he* who was feeling inferior, perhaps thinking: *"How can I, Chairman of this and Director of that, be so useless at playing this instrument? This young teacher must be thinking I'm wasting her time!"* Or, if a teacher felt intimidated teaching an aggressive adolescent, she may miss the possibility that it was *he* who was feeling intimidated, perhaps desperately worried about *her* approval of *him*: *"I'm going to show her! She's going to think I'm cool!"*

We may also *mistakenly* attribute our feelings to the pupil, positive or negative. Our feelings are not always the pupil's feelings. So, as well as using countertransference, we also need to be informed by what we observe about the pupil (through facial expression, body language, actions, words and silences) and by what we know about the causes of negative energy in pupils.

Common Causes of Negative Energy in Pupils

The more usual causes of negative energy from pupils are (the first four points have been dealt with in more detail in Chapters One, Two and Three):

Feeling unable or being unable to do it: Having a lack of inner resource, feeling insufficiently supported, anxious and helpless.

Not wanting to do it: Being uninterested, or feeling the pace is too slow or feeling pushed and rushed, resulting in disinterest, boredom, frustration, resentment, humiliation, anger and wanting to block learning etc.

Any negative transference: If verbalised, some examples could be:

"My parents can't handle my fearful feelings, so you won't be able to either. So I'll stay safely buttoned up inside myself and not contribute." (Untrusting)

"My teachers never think I'm good enough, so you won't either." (Fearful)

"I'm never allowed to learn what I want. So you won't let me either."

"You look like my nasty Aunt Mary, so you'll be like her." (Hostile)

Having no idea how to be a "good" pupil: Having never internalised "good" behaviour either through having no such role model from the home, or through being insufficiently socially aware to pick up such cues from home or school.

Having unhelpful habits in learning: For example, *habitually* doing as little as can be got away with, *expecting* to take a back seat, *resisting* anything new, or *reacting aggressively* to teaching. Very often, such unhelpful habits are rooted in one or more significant emotional events in early childhood in which the child felt threatened and reacted *defensively* for emotional and psychological survival. The initial defence then becomes that person's habitual response and can be summed up as:

fright: entrenchment in the existing position, resistance to learning

flight: not being fully present in mind or body, evasion of learning

fight: anger or aggression, which may be uncontrolled and unhelpful, or which *may* result in positive effort.

Not wanting to change, preferring to keep the existing self-image: For example, a non-successful pupil may realise that if he were to succeed he might have to work harder to keep his new place amongst his peers, and he might have to cope with their feelings of envy. Also, he would have to change his own self-image. He might then *prefer* to remain with his accustomed: *"Poor me, I find it so hard!"* self-image, *comfortably* not progressing.

Having a vested interest in not progressing, typically to prove a point: For example, a pupil's parent might unduly coerce the pupil into lessons and practice, perhaps unconsciously seeking to fulfil her own musical potential through the child. The child's only defence is then not to cooperate: *"I'm only here because I have to be. You can make me come but you can't make me learn."* Or: *"I may be able to do it, but I'm not going to give you the pleasure and satisfaction of my achievement".*

Not being "present": Something in the lesson can trigger an irrelevant but emotionally engaging train of thought causing the pupil, quite suddenly and unexpectedly, to "go away" from what is being taught.

Countertransference: picking up the teacher's negative feelings: Just as we can pick up the pupil's feelings, so the pupil can pick up our feelings. We need to be aware of our own feelings, especially negative ones, and their effects on pupils.

Being Aware of Our Own Feelings and their Effects on Pupils

One of the easiest ways of being aware of our own feelings, and their effects on our pupils, is to be aware of our thoughts. Let's look at the given Pupil B examples to explore this:

The first given example B's thoughts:

"We must get on."

"It'll never be ready in time."

"What will the parents think?"

"If the examiners ... or audience ... hears it like this they'll think I'm a useless teacher!"

"He ought to do these scales and exercises."

"He ought not to play by ear."

"Help! I can't teach jazz improvisation! So we won't do it!"

"Why can't he just practise as I showed him? Then he'd be able to do it."

From this we can see that this teacher feels internally pressured. She feels pressured by time and the need to produce results. She feels pressured by what other significant people (parents, examiners and audiences) will think of her teaching. She feels pressured by her own internalised authority figures or the "received wisdom" she has in her head from her conventional music education. She also feels pressured, or perhaps persecuted, by her own feelings of inadequacy or "not being able", and by the fact that the pupil is not learning in *her* way. When she feels such internal pressure, she can hardly help but pressurise the pupil, consciously or unconsciously "pushing" him.

Internally pressured teachers tend to be directive teachers

Internally pressured teachers tend to be very conscientious and take full responsibility for the pupil's progress. They may feel accountable to parents, teachers, past professors and the musical authority figures in their heads. They may prefer the pupil only to learn music with which they are familiar and, preferably, in *their* way. Put yourself in the pupil's shoes:

What might you like and what might you dislike about such directive teaching?

Now let's consider the second given example B's thoughts:

"I wonder what he'll come up with this week!"

"I'll just observe and see how he tackles it."

"It takes as long as it takes; he'll be ready when he's ready."

"He'll never be able to learn this ... I'll never be able to teach it to him."

"He hasn't practised again. I'm not going to bother myself."

"It's his responsibility, it's up to him."

"When's break?"

"zzzzzzzzzzzzzzzzzzzzzzzzzzzzzzzzzzzzzzzzzzzz"!

This teacher typifies the opposite extreme. Far from feeling pressured, she is clearly very relaxed with both herself and her pupils.

Relaxed teachers usually teach in a non-directive way

Relaxed teachers usually teach in a non-directive way allowing the pupil to choose his own music, set his own goals, direct his own learning and identify his own problems. They allow him to tackle learning in his own time and in his own way. Put yourself in the pupil's shoes:

What might you like and what might you dislike about such non-directive teaching?

Now consider the thoughts you had as you taught Pupil B (i) and B (ii). Think about the inner feelings that drove them: What effect could they have had on your teaching and your pupils?

Pupil B (i):

Pupil B (ii):

Did you find you were a predominantly directive or non-directive teacher?

Perhaps you noticed that your teaching changes depending on who and what you are teaching? In any event, we need to be aware that *it may be our own thoughts,* if too pressured and directive, or if too casual and non-directive, *which actually cause negative energy* in lessons.

Common Causes of Negative Energy in Teachers and the Effects on Pupils

Internal pressures

It is only too easy for us to feel internally pressured given the constraints of our situation, but this may make us lose touch with what and how we would *like* to teach, and put undue pressure on the pupil:

Time pressure: We are under immense time pressure. Lessons usually have to be short, but learning to play an instrument is enormously complicated.

Pressure to produce results: We may feel under pressure to produce results in exams, concerts and festivals or to produce results for parents, the Head of Music or Education Authority etc.

The pressure of many different pupils in quick succession: Having many pupils of differing ability in quick succession requires us to be constantly adjusting our pace, or interrupting our flow. A quick pupil after a slow one requires a sudden boost in energy, but a slow pupil after a quick one can be particularly difficult as it tends to be harder for us to slow down than speed up. Also, especially at the beginning of any teaching relationship, it can be only too easy for us to overestimate a pupil both through transference and through wanting him to feel successful: *"He looks a bright, he won't have any problems with this, he'll enjoy it!"* Overestimation results in mutual discomfort and a need to change down a gear while also trying to save the pupil's face. Underestimation can be easier to correct, but both can cause pressure.

Internal fears

Our fears can also adversely affect our teaching by constricting us so that we cannot be open to the pupil and his interests and needs. Typical fears are:

- "Not being able" or "not knowing how" to teach something: *"Help! I can't teach imrovisation ... or that concerto ... so we won't do it".* In trying to protect ourselves, we may block the pupil.
- Fear of our own internalised authority figures, especially previous music teachers: *"It's not right to play by ear ... or play pop music ... we <u>ought</u> to be doing scales and exercises".*

  We tend to teach as we were taught, feeling safest that way. It's what we know, and can do, and it came from an authority figure. We may then feel very unsure of anything else and unprepared to be open to the pupil's interests if they don't fall in line with ours.
- Fear of being directive or non-directive: Also, through transference, we can fear being directive. If conscious, the fear could be verbalised as: *"Being firm will result in the pupil feeling disrespected. He will resent it, dislike me and run away".* Or, through transference, we can fear being non-directive: *"Unless I insist on the pupil doing it in my way, now, he will have no respect for me and nothing will happen at all".* Either of these may be unhelpful to the pupil's current needs.
- Fears when our pupils perform: Our fears *for* our pupils in performance situations, and *of* parent's expectations and what other teachers or examiners may think, can be a severe source of stress. We may feel increased anxiety and that increased anxiety may be transferred onto the pupil.

Our own internal pressures and fears prevent us from responding to the pupil

In a nutshell, it's our own internal pressures, fears, transferences, preconceived ideas and also, our personal preoccupations, which prevent us from picking up the cues and keying into the pupil's interests and needs. In these ways we, quite unwittingly, contribute to negative energy. So what can we do to maintain positive energy?

Maintaining Positive Energy: Practical Suggestions

Feeling secure within ourselves

We need to feel secure enough in ourselves and in our own professionalism to cope with our internal pressures and fears, whatever they may be. It is only if we feel such security that we can be fully present and engaged and respond to the pupil and his interests and needs.

Knowing our own teaching philosophy

For this it can be very helpful to be clear about our own personal teaching philosophy, knowing *consciously* what is important to us in our teaching and why.

Think about your personal teaching philosophy: What is important to you in your teaching and why? Then fill in the box below:

Example of a personal teaching philosophy:

First, it is important to me that my pupils enjoy their lessons as I know that it is only if they are enjoying themselves that they will be fully engaged with what they are doing, and so be learning as effectively as they can. It is also important to me that they enjoy lessons because then, through positive emotional association, they will want to come back for more and continue learning into adulthood (either with me, or another teacher or by themselves).

Second, it is important to me that my pupils realise their own goals, learning to read music, play by ear or improvise: whatever most interests them so that they feel they are going where *they* want to go.

Third it is important to me that I try to inspire them, spark their interest and educate them by introducing them to many different musical styles and skills.

Fourth, as far as my pupils are able and willing, I like to ensure that they always have something they can play *now* (a piece or improvisation) with or, preferably, without the written music, so that they can enjoy playing spontaneously, anywhere, any time.

Maintaining an open, flexible and positive attitude

We also need to maintain an open, flexible and positive attitude to our teaching:

We need to be open to new experience and able to change our views in the light of new experience and we need to be able to see beyond our existing skills, constantly enriching and enhancing them (The very fact that you are reading these words is evidence of your ability to be open in this way).

Also, as through countertransference our pupils can pick up *our* feelings experiencing them as their own feelings, it is important that we maintain a positive attitude. However, we may need to take care that we don't become so excited and wrapped up in what we are teaching that we leave the pupil behind feeling: *"She's off again!"* Or *"Help! I can't keep up!"*

"Trust yourself, trust the pupil and trust the process" is a good psychological maxim.

Dealing with Negative Feeling

Some negative feeling or energy is an inevitable part of the learning process (as described more fully in Chapter One) and it is unrealistic not to be ready for it.

Unobtrusively: tracking and shifting energy

As far as possible it is preferable to deal with it unobtrusively, subtly responding to the pupil so that he never feels either stuck in negativity or obviously rescued.

Remembering that positive energy relies on a mutual flow between teacher and pupil we may need to "empower" the pupil both by maintaining "unconditional positive regard" and by constantly staying in touch with what and how he really wants to learn.

Using countertransference, observation and our knowledge of likely feeling, we need to "track" feeling, being fully aware of all those subtle, fleeting, feeling impressions, the pupil's excitement, interests, fears, muddles, difficulties and blocks, as they ebb and flow. We need to be ready to change tack or shift activity to something the pupil enjoys, and can do, when positive energy is waning (See Chapter Five).

Especially for blocked or frustrated feelings (as in the first given example B), we could stand back, let go and enable the pupil to set his own goals, direct his own learning defining his own problems and go at his own pace. On the other hand, where there is helpless and confused feeling (as in the second given example B), we may need to "contain" the pupil, being directive, breaking the task down to its smallest component parts, taking one simple bite-sized task at a time and rewarding, praising and encouraging every achievement. In both of these cases handling the feeling involved changes the energy flow between teacher and pupil.

Finally, as, through countertransference, our feelings and therefore our needs are likely to be mutual, a useful tip can be to give the pupil whatever we feel we need ourselves. For example, if we feel vulnerable, we need to *give* reassurance; if we feel rushed, we need to give time; if we feel muddled or too full, we need to give space and room for digestion.

Use your own feeling
(countertransference)
to maintain good feeling

IF IT FEELS:

Blocked, frustrating
Let the pupil lead, and use "right brain":

- Ask what they want to learn.
- Ask them to identify their own difficulties, ask questions, and try to find their own solutions
- Focus on feeling, imagery and imagination
- Improvise, play by ear or use the whole body: Sing, clap, step

Or just change activity

IF IT FEELS:

Helpless, confusing
Take charge, reassure, and use "left brain":

- Be a *Caring Parent*, reassure
- Remind them of their achievements and what they *can* do
- Frame the difficulty: "It's from here to here", break it down into bite-sized steps, and do one step at a time
- Do it *with* them, playing together slowly and securely, until it feels and sounds good

In discussion: using counselling skills

If positive energy can't be restored unobtrusively, we need to enter a discussion. For this, skills commonly used by counsellors can be enormously helpful:

Allow time and a safe space: Both teacher and pupil need to have time and space to tune in and explore feelings, and options, in safety.

Be unfailingly empathic, accepting the pupil's feelings without judgement even when they feel threatening: It is important that we don't ignore, run away from or try to fix or mend the pupil's feelings. By allowing them as they are, we "hold" them for him, so that he can fully experience and become conscious of them. Then, *he* (not we) can more easily decide what to do to resolve them.

"Meet" the pupil's feeling: Using both observation and countertransference we can gauge the pupil's feeling and "meet" it, as we feel appropriate, by saying for example:

"I'm wondering if this feels too much (or too difficult or too dull or too frustrating) for today?"

Or: "I'm feeling rather tired (or anxious or bored or angry) ... how about you?"

Or: "I'm feeling at a loss ... there's something wrong isn't there?"

If the feeling has been sensitively and accurately judged and acceptingly and non-judgementally expressed, the pupil will feel relieved: *"She understands!"*. More often than not this will result in an immediate shift in feeling. It may also lead to helpful, open discussion.

Reflect and paraphrase: In the same way, it can also be very helpful if the teacher gently reflects and paraphrases any feeling the pupil expresses. This enables the pupil to feel heard and it enables the teacher to check for understanding. Perhaps most importantly, it also enables the pupil to see his own problem with clarity and objectivity thus helping him know how to deal with it. For example:

Pupil: *"It just seems so huge and difficult!"*

Teacher: *"Huge and difficult. A lot for you to take on".* (Reflecting)

Pupil's internal response:

"Yes! It is. Okay, I can see that clearly now. It is a lot, but I still want to do it".

Ask "open" questions: These are questions which cannot be answered by "yes" or "no" and so are useful in eliciting feelings (they usually begin *"How"* or *"What")*. For example:

"How do you feel about your playing at the moment?"

"What would you like to do about the exam right now?"

"I'm wondering how you're feeling ... what you're thinking ... right now."

Using words such as "*at the moment*" and *"right now"* reduces the long term negativity, and this enables the pupil to feel free to give expression to how he is feeling *now,* with both of you knowing that he may or may not *always* feel like that, and is free to shift in the way he feels.

Remain open: Trust the right solution to emerge in its own time out of the discussion

An example of a discussion between teacher and pupil using counselling skills:

Silence, a non-cooperative atmosphere.

Teacher: Resisting the urge to step in and make things happen, as it's clear the pupil doesn't want to cooperate, but trying to tune in to the pupil's feelings, respecting his *need* to be the way he is:

"I'm wondering how you're feeling right now, whether you want to be here today?" (gently and empathically "meeting" the feeling).

Pupil: Shrugs ever so slightly but doesn't look at the teacher. (If he had looked at the teacher she might have empathically reflected his shrugging gesture and expression back to him).

Teacher: *"Really bad, uh?"* (Reflecting)

Pupil: Silent.

Teacher: Allows the silence, doesn't break into it, and continues to try to tune in with the pupil's feelings, supporting and "containing" them. After a long pause:

"I'm wondering if you want to tell me about it? Perhaps part of you wants to but something is stopping you?" (More or less open question)

Pupil: Now feeling sufficiently secure in the teacher's empathic rapport:

"You don't understand!" (Making a transference from previous authority figures that no-one understands him, listens to him or lets him do what he wants):

"I don't want to be here at all! I'm made to be here and I don't like music and I don't want to play."

Teacher: Steadfastly refusing to feel threatened but focusing on the pupil:

"You feel <u>made</u> to come and you don't like any of it.." ("Meeting" the feeling, reflecting and paraphrasing)

Pupil: Now that his feelings have been "met", he feels lighter, less entrenched and realises it's not *all* bad:

"Well I don't mind <u>you,</u> but I'd rather do something else".

The conversation is now more secure. The pupil is talking so the teacher can ask more open and focusing questions such as: *"Who is making you come? Do you know why?" "Did you have something particular in mind you'd rather do?" "Would you like to discontinue music altogether, or is there any aspect of it you enjoy?" "Would you like me to speak to your parents about it?"* In this way the teacher can find out whether it is really appropriate for the pupil to give up, or whether some modification or compromise in lessons would be appropriate.

Dealing with aggression or anger

Conversations that start with the pupil refusing to cooperate are not uncommon as, in our society, we tend not to express anger overtly but covertly, digging a trench with it, getting in and refusing to come out.

If the pupil is overtly aggressive and does express anger overtly, we are likely to feel very threatened, both through the direct threat and through countertransference, as an angry person usually feels threatened underneath. In this case we must resist the temptation either to get angry in response or to collapse under the fear. Instead we need to accept his feelings as his, look him in the eye and be able to "contain" or "hold" him. We could then meet and reflect his feelings verbally: *"You're feeling very angry about it".* Or: *"It's making you feel very angry".* Having feelings met and reflected in this way usually takes the wind out of the aggressor's sails and enables calmer discussion.

Parting

Like all people, pupils can be very complex, having a variety of conflicting motivational forces within them, some conscious and some unconscious. We can't change them. A pupil will only cooperate and learn if he *wants* to, and we should see this as a reflection of the pupil himself, not of our teaching, while also doing what we can as teachers.

Not all pupils are suited to music and not all teachers are suited to all pupils. (I don't think there's one football coach in this world who could persuade me to enjoy football lessons, much less to *practise* football!) When, having reasonably tried everything, positive energy is still not forthcoming in lessons, agreeing to part may be the right and the only thing to do. It might also be a relief to both teacher and pupil!

We need to remember that we are teachers not counsellors, trained as teachers not counsellors and being paid to teach not counsel. We can use counselling skills to help maintain and restore positive energy for learning, but some pupils' problems may be well beyond our scope. In these cases, we can only try to refer them on to the help they need through discussion with their parents and their school teachers.

Summary and Practical Checklist

MAINTAINING POSITIVE ENERGY

Dealing with Negative Feeling

- Positive energy in lessons is the result of a mutual flow of energy between teacher and pupil. When this happens, teaching feels like creation in action.
- Be aware of the quality of energy in the lesson through countertransference, observation and through knowing the likely causes of negative feeling in pupils.
- Be aware of yourself, not only your feelings but also your thoughts as you teach, and their likely effect on pupils. In particular, be aware of your internal pressures, fears, transferences, preconceived ideas and preoccupations.
- Maintain your own inner security through knowing your personal teaching philosophy, and by having an open, flexible and positive attitude to your teaching.
- Trust yourself, trust the pupil and trust the process.
- "Empower" the pupil by giving "unconditional positive regard".
- "Track" feeling, notice where the energy is perking or where it is beginning to ebb, be aware of all feelings: excitement, fear, stress, frustration, muddle, confusion, helplessness, hopelessness, boredom, disinterest, "absence" etc.
- Shift activity to something the pupil enjoys and can do when positive energy is waning (see Chapter Five).
- "Contain" feeling, especially the fear of not being able to do it. For helpless and confused feeling try being directive, isolating the problem, breaking it down to its smallest component parts, taking one simple bite-sized task at a time and rewarding, praising and encouraging every achievement
- For blocked or frustrated feelings: Let go! Enable the pupil to set his own goals, direct his own learning, defining his own problems and going at his own pace.
- Give to the pupil whatever you feel *you* need as, through countertransference, your feelings and therefore your needs are likely to be mutual. For example, if you feel stressed or rushed give the pupil space, if you feel vulnerable give the pupil reassurance.

In discussion

- Allow time and a safe space.
- Respect and accept the pupil's feelings, allow them, including the feelings that feel threatening to you.
- "Sit" with the feelings, hold them for the pupil to look at and resolve himself. Don't collapse, don't get angry, don't criticise and don't try to fix or mend them for him.
- "Meet" feeling sensitively with gentle open-ended statements or questions.
- Gently reflect and paraphrase feelings.
- Ask open questions: usually questions that begin: "What" or "How".
- Remain open. Trust the right solution to emerge in its own time out of the discussion.

Personal Reflection

MAINTAINING POSITIVE ENERGY

Dealing with Negative Feeling

Reflect briefly on the contents of the chapter. Make a note of the points of particular interest to you below. Then, compile your personal practical checklist on the following page.

Finally, visualise yourself putting any new ideas from your checklist into practice.

Personal Practical Checklist

MAINTAINING POSITIVE ENERGY

Dealing with Negative Feeling

Chapter Five: Making Music Now

Practical Activities to Have Fun and Raise Energy

"My work is to empower people through the creative process.

I expect that others are just like me: they want to wake up; they want to be set free".

Gabrielle Roth, Maps to Ecstasy, 1989

Making Music Now

Many pupils begin lessons because they want to make music and they want to make it *now*. But even with the best of teachers and the best of intentions, owing to the emotional demands, the number of skills required and the conventional, intellectual educational bias, learning to play an instrument can sometimes feel difficult and lack musical satisfaction. Practice can feel like an arid chore, best avoided.

But, whether they practise or not, it is clearly evident that pupils enjoy *playing*. They tinker and "mess about" especially on keyboards. They play Chopsticks, Blue Moon or the latest TV jingle unstoppably, making up all sorts of homemade variations, for fun. Without realising it, while doing this, they are gaining in aural skills, finger dexterity, understanding of the instrument and a host of general musicianship skills. Hence the suggestions below as a quick lift for when energy is low, or just for fun:

Moving

Physical movement helps relax and centre pupils in their bodies and so helps them to be fully present and engaged, rather than anxiously in their heads, hoping to get it right or wishing they were somewhere else. Physical movement also helps pupils internalise musical elements such as pulse, rhythm, pitch, phrase length, musical quality etc. (see Chapter Two: Whole Body Skills).

So: Change position, shrug, clap, click, tap, step, stamp, jump, dance, laugh!

Playing Together

The pupil can feel enormous emotional and musical support and enhanced musical satisfaction if the teacher, with her rounder, richer, more mature musical skills, plays *with* the pupil. This could be whatever he is studying, or duets, ensembles, well-known and familiar tunes, or on-the-spot improvisation.

Improvising

The point about improvisation is that it provides instant musical satisfaction. It's important to keep the parameters of the improvisation well within the pupils' capabilities otherwise the point is lost and it is no fun! If in doubt, err on the easier side and adjust upwards. Some suggestions:

- **Copy me:** Teacher and pupil take it in turns to make up anything from very short snippets to long phrases and copy each other. The notes used could be very clearly defined at first, for example, just the first three notes that the pupil learnt to play, or just open strings, or just the pentatonic scale (black notes). If on a piano or keyboard, the teacher could do this over a rhythmic ostinato bass pattern in the left hand (for example, alternating tonic and dominant or simple open fifth and open sixth chords).
- **Question and Answer:** Extending "Copy Me": Teacher and pupil take it in turns to play the musical question, the other player then answers it.
- **Reflection and Communication:** The teacher listens closely to the pupil, reflecting feelings and ideas, playing supportively. The teacher could then not only reflect, but also initiate, according to her own feeling, so that there is a dialogue of feeling in which both teacher and pupil can sometimes initiate and sometimes respond, as desired.
- **On whatever you're teaching:** For example, if you are teaching new notes, scales, chords or rhythmic patterns, the pupil could perhaps start learning the new material through the "Copy Me" or "Question and Answer" above. Then he could improvise freely with the new material, perhaps over the teacher playing an underlying rhythmic or ostinato pattern. In this way, because of the ongoing musical impetus, particularly if accompanied, pupils *enjoy* playing anything, including scales (or parts of scales) for *longer* than they would otherwise. Also, because the pupil is interacting with the new material and using it creatively (rather than just reading it off the page), it helps him to assimilate and *"own"* it more effectively.
- **Something Fixed, Something Free:** Teacher and pupil choose parameters or boundaries within which to improvise. Setting parameters can, paradoxically, facilitate greater freedom: if there are no parameters players can feel helplessly lost, not knowing where to start, but if parameters are set in areas where the players feel confident, they then have the confidence to explore the parameters to the full.

  The following (and any other) parameters could be set and used, one or more at a time:

  - **Two or three notes:** C and G, or C D Eb, or G A B etc.
  - **Comfortable and interesting five-finger positions** e.g. CDEFG (major), ABCDE (minor), GA CDE, (inverted major pentatonic), C Eb F F# G (blues)
  - **Scales or Keys:** Pentatonic, modes (Dorian, Aeolian etc.), majors, minors, whole tone, jazz, blues, Jewish, Arabian etc.
  - **Single note accompaniments:** Alternating tonic and dominant; open strings; four note ostinato (repeated) patterns for example in C Major: C, E, F, G or C, F, A, G; descending chromatics; down a fifth, up a fourth until the lower tonic has been reached.
  - **Alternating melody and accompaniment with two players:** Players take turns to improvise a melody and play a simple held note or ostinato accompaniment. For example, the first player could improvise a melody for eight counts and then play the accompaniment, while the second player first plays the accompaniment for eight counts and then improvises a melody.

- o **Chords:** Open fifth and open sixth chords e.g. CG and CA in C major. Chords I, IV and V7 in comfortable inversions e.g. CEG (I), CFA (IV) and BFG (V7) in C major.
- o **Chord progressions:** I, I, V, I, or I, VI, IV, V, or II7, V7, I , or the twelve bar blues, or selecting a four chord progression from the piece of music that the pupil is studying.
- o **Modulations:** C major, modulating to A minor (or other closely related key) and back.
- o **Time Signatures:** 2/4, 3/4, 4/4, 6/8, 9/8 etc.
- o **Rhythms:** Lullaby, waltz, calypso, march.
- o **Moods:** Contemplative, joyful, dancing, etc.
- o **Phrase or structural shapes:** AABA or ABAB or ABACA etc.

- **On a theme:** For example: "A Thunderstorm", "Beside the Sea", "Going to the Park"
- **Illustrating a picture with music:** The pupil could bring his own picture, perhaps one he has drawn or painted, or one he has searched online, or the teacher could have a book of pictures or postcards from which the pupil could choose. They could discuss the picture trying out illustrations (for example: sunshine or rain music, growing trees or singing birds music, or skipping, running or jumping music as appropriate to the picture), and then "performing" it together.
- **Narrating and illustrating a poem or Haiku**
- **Narrating and illustrating a story with music:** Teacher and pupil could take it in turns to make up and illustrate a story. For example:

Teacher: *"Once there was a 9-year-old boy, who hated practising scales"* then playing scales badly and without interest, with the pupil joining in.

Pupil: "So he ran out into the garden and hid behind a tree" then playing "running and hiding" music with the teacher joining in.

Teacher: *"Where he was suddenly startled by a tiny mewing sound"* then playing tiny mewing sounds with the pupil joining in.

Pupil: *"And saw a tiny kitten stuck in the branches"* then playing kittenish music with the teacher joining in.

Continuing until a natural conclusion is reached.

- **Expressing current feelings through playing:** Especially difficult feelings (for example: frustration, anger or helplessness) using the music as therapy.
- **Completely freely**: No guidelines or boundaries, teacher and pupil play freely responding to each other.

Graphic Notation

Graphic, or "homemade", notation can be used to compose and then play music, or to write down music that has just been improvised. Rather than conveying pitch, rhythm and other musical elements exactly, graphic notation is an aide memoire, conveying overall shape, texture and musical expression in a graphic manner, using pencil or colours and a piece of paper. Each performance from graphic notation is likely to differ, therefore, from every other performance. It allows for wide ranging musical expression and is easy to use, and fun! Many pupils will be familiar with it having used it in class music lessons at school.

The ideas in this chapter are included in a practical form in Piano by Ear (Please click on the image to visit webpage with further information):

Personal Reflection

MAKING MUSIC NOW

Practical Activities to Have Fun and Raise Energy

Reflect briefly on the contents of the chapter. Make a note of the points of particular interest to you below. Then, compile your personal practical checklist on the following page.

Finally, visualise yourself putting any new ideas from your checklist into practice.

Personal Practical Checklist

MAKING MUSIC NOW

Practical Activities to Have Fun and Raise Energy

Chapter Six: Group Teaching

"Growth is a process of experimentation, a series of trials, errors and occasional victories. The failed experiments are as much part of the process as the experiments that work."

Cherie Carter-Scott,

If Life is a Game, These are the Rules, 1998

Exploring How to Teach in Groups

Group instrumental music teaching is comparatively new in our society, born more out of economic necessity than choice. As a result, many of us teaching in groups have not experienced being taught in a group. We are feeling in the dark, learning by trial and error, and experimenting. We know when our experimentation is successful because *then* we feel we *want* to continue teaching in groups, even if we no longer *have* to.

Advantages of Group Music Lessons

Group lessons can help pupils feel the connection between their instrumental playing and the wider world of music making. They can be more fun as pupils experience the joy of playing together and, in having to play together, pupils can more swiftly develop an appreciation of pitch, rhythm and other musical qualities. Group lessons can also be mutually supportive, lessening both the isolation and the anxiety associated with one-to-one lessons, and pupils can learn from each other. Finally, the wish for the group to succeed or the fear of letting the group down (or of letting oneself down in front of peers), can help ensure that practice is done.

For the teacher, though, group teaching requires more forethought and preparation, and classroom management skills.

Overlapping Lessons

If it's not possible to teach in groups, perhaps because there's no time available or because parents are unable or unprepared to bring children twice a week, consider overlapping lessons. This way each pupil can have a longer lesson, overlapping perhaps with both the pupil who comes before and the one who comes after, so benefitting from mutual support and from hearing and learning from what others are doing. Matching pupils for standard and ability may be helpful, but it's not necessary. Younger pupils can benefit enormously from hearing older ones, so gaining a clearer idea of what they're aiming for, and older pupils can learn a huge amount, re-enforcing their own skills and knowledge, by hearing and helping younger ones. It is less easy to successfully mix groups in which younger pupils are more advanced than older ones.

Sibling Rivalry

Just as the infant and growing child needs to feel special to the parent, never mind how many siblings there are, so each pupil needs to feel special to his teacher. Especially in our competitive society, where so many of us confuse being *able* with being *loved*, the pupil may be wondering how he compares with our other pupils: Is he one of the best, and therefore extra dear? Or the worst and so, possibly, not wanted?

Owing to the very presence of peers, there will be "sibling rivalry" in group lessons, arising out of each pupil's need to be special to us. Each pupil is also likely to need to feel accepted by and a necessary part of the group. We need to be aware of how they seek to achieve this: Through good behaviour? Through trying not to be noticed (feeling that to be safer than being exposed and found wanting)? Through being comical? Or disruptive? Disruption may be motivated by not wanting to do it, fearing not being able to do it, feeling that doing it is irrelevant or by needing to be noticed by us.

We need to make sure that each group member feels that they are cared for, accepted and appreciated by us and that we have our mind around them. We need to be particularly aware that criticism, especially if too harsh or unjustified, to a group member in front of a group member can feel very painful and humiliating and perhaps frighten the pupil away for life.

Emotionally Demanding Behaviour

Typically, individuals within groups demand firstly by needing our undivided attention and approval, and secondly by being disruptive. In both cases the underlying motivation is likely to be a need to feel better about themselves, to feel more internally secure, which is why, through countertransference, we are likely to feel supremely insecure when met with disruption. In both cases such a pupil could benefit from having his behaviour gently and empathetically reflected, or mirrored, back to him:

> *"It seems you'd like lots of reassurance today, Phil!"*

Or: *"It seems you want to disrupt the whole class today, David"*.

Helping the pupil see his own behaviour in this way helps him to be conscious of it so that, rather than acting out in response to his unconscious motivation or in response to what he *thinks* we will think, he can begin to behave as he would *like* himself to be, which, in most cases, is in a socially acceptable manner.

Also, in both cases, the pupil may benefit from having his own "Inner Carer" strengthened. Although the degree to which our pupils can *hear* our praise and reassurance varies, by giving praise ourselves, and by encouraging mutual support, appreciation and encouragement amongst pupils, all pupils can be helped to internalise positive things about themselves and thus strengthen their "Inner Carers" (see Chapter One).

Differing Abilities

Very few pupils in group music lessons are exactly matched for ability. We are always having to find ways of simultaneously engaging and educating pupils of widely differing musical backgrounds, interests and abilities. Below are some suggestions:

> **Group directed lessons:** Encourage the group, as appropriate to their ages, to set their own goals (for example learning certain tunes to play on certain occasions?) and their own rules of behaviour. Feeling an intrinsic part of the process helps each group member to feel a valuable and necessary part of the whole, and fosters cooperation both between themselves and between themselves and the teacher.
>
> **Use their skills to help you:** Have pupils help each other. Learning is more thoroughly assimilated if the learnt skill is then taught, and if some of the pupils are teaching or testing others. The teacher is then free to attend where most needed.
>
> **Use worksheets:** Have tasks ready to occupy some pupils while attending to others, for example, have pencil and paper worksheets of key signatures, rhythmic patterns, pitches, or have them compose a piece of music in their own graphic notation (a simpler aide memoire than conventional notation).
>
> **Use the group for supportive concert experience:** Encourage pupils to perform to each other in the group, perhaps having each group member then say one positive and supportive comment to the person who has just played. This helps develop confidence both in the one who has just performed, and in the one who has commented for when he plays later.
>
> **Use the competitive element:** Properly handled, group lessons can engender more practice. Many pupils may feel their warm and kindly individual teacher will not make them feel too awful for lack of practice, but who wants to be shown up in front of their peers? And who wants to be the one to let the group down? Have pupils prepare and play whatever needs to be practised to each other: scales, pieces, the difficult bits.
>
> Educational games, with a gently competitive element, can be beneficial and fun too.

Write, adapt or arrange music to suit their different skills.

Make music together: Play, have fun, improvise! (See Chapter Five)

Personal Reflection

GROUP TEACHING

Reflect briefly on the contents of the chapter. Make a note of the points of particular interest to you below. Then, compile your personal practical checklist on the following page.

Finally, visualise yourself putting any new ideas from your checklist into practice.

Personal Practical Checklist

GROUP TEACHING

Chapter Seven: Parents

"Dialogue is a creative, involving experience, which aims to produce a useful outcome for both participants. The interaction is genuinely two-way, like people dancing or playing music together. People take turns, connect with each other and approach the conversation with an open mind."

Gerard Egan and Andrew Bailey,

TalkWorks at work, 2000

EXERCISE: EXPLORING TEACHER-PUPIL-PARENT RELATIONSHIPS

- As a pupil, what did you want:
  - (a) From your parent:
    - Aged 4-10
    - Aged 11-18
  - (b) From your teacher:
  - (c) For yourself:
- As a parent what do you (or would you) want:
  - (a) For your child as pupil:
  - (b) From the teacher:
  - (c) (c)For yourself (as parent):
- As the teacher what do you want:
  - (a) For and from your pupil:
  - (b) From the parent:
  - (c) For yourself:

EXERCISE WORKSHEET: EXPLORING TEACHER-PUPIL-PARENT RELATIONSHIPS

- As a pupil, what did you want:
  - (a) From your parent:
    - Aged 4-10
    - Aged 11-18
  - (b) From your teacher:
  - (c) For yourself:
- As a parent what do you (or would you) want:
  - (a) For your child as pupil:
  - (b) From the teacher:
  - (c) For yourself (as parent):
- As the teacher what do you want:
  - (a) For and from your pupil:
  - (b) From the parent:
  - (c) For yourself:

Teachers, Pupils and Parents

The working relationships between teacher, pupil and parent naturally varies depending upon the teaching methods being used, and the personalities involved. To establish the best possible relationship, it can be helpful to understand the psychological and emotional factors between pupils and parents, and between teachers and parents.

Understanding Pupils and Parents

Parent as Caregiver and Critic

As discussed in Chapter One, the parent is the pupil's first, and therefore most powerful, caregiver and authority figure –the ultimate authority. The child looks to the parent for the care, warmth and appreciation that he needs, and because he believes his parent knows everything, and is always right –especially about himself and his place in the world, parental appreciation is especially powerful and life-enhancing. Likewise, parental criticism can be especially powerful and annihilating.

Parent as Caregiver

It goes without saying that the child needs the parent's care, warmth and appreciation for music learning and practice. As described in earlier chapters, practice entails the coordination of many complicated and differing skills and it may easily be accompanied by the child *feeling* anxious, *feeling* that he cannot do it successfully. Even the thought of practice can be putting off if the pupil is not sure that he knows what to do, or how to succeed in doing it. So it is very important that parents make the right kind of comments. Also, the right kind of comments can then be internalised by the pupil to become what he says inside his head to support himself –his "Inner Carer" (more below). Here are some suggestions:

"That sounded lovely!"

"Well done! That is coming on!"

"At this rate you'll be able to do it in no time!"

"That bit feels hard, doesn't it? So what about trying just the tiniest bit from there to there?"

"If you do just five more minutes you can have a drink and a snack."

Parent as Ultimate Authority or Critic: Life Giver or Annihilator

If the parent, perhaps through feeling responsible or anxious for results, neglects the caregiving and appreciative role and instead assumes the authority role by trying to "teach" or by, however inadvertently, criticising, the child may feel not only that his support system has gone, but that there is added anxiety to an already pressured situation. This may provoke, quite unexpectedly and, seemingly, out of all proportion to the situation, a terrified temper tantrum or flat refusal. (The child may also feel free to give way to such emotions in front of the parent, whereas he is less likely to feel either that he wants to or that he is able to in front of the teacher).

Understanding Pupils and Parents

Child / Pupil **Parent**

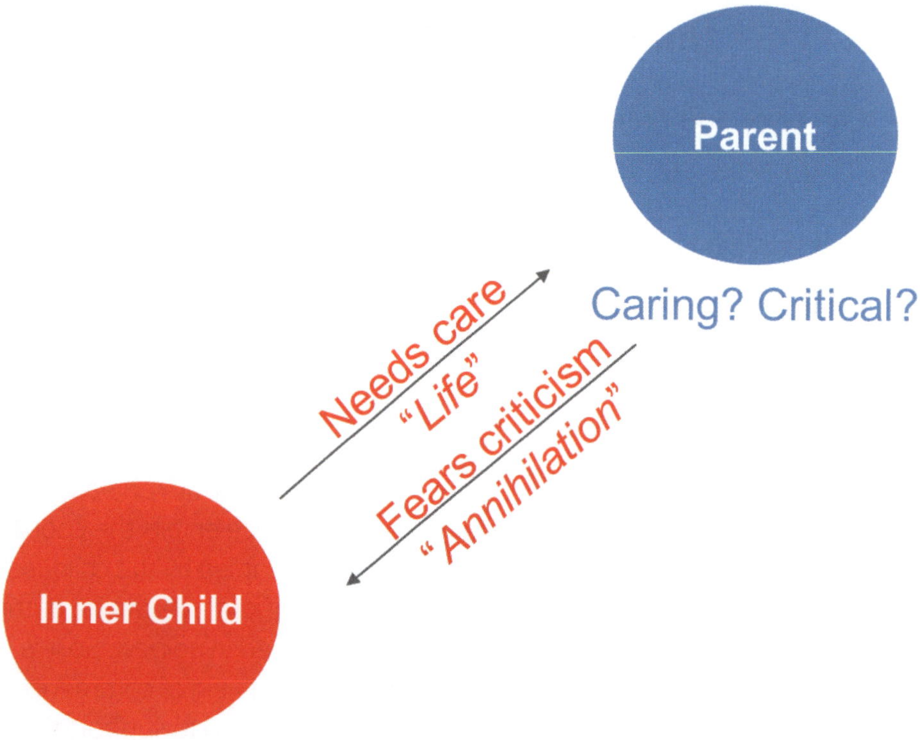

Needs appreciation and approval.
If criticised, is likely to feel
threatened, angry and defensive

Above all, children need appreciation and approval from their parents. If parents, perhaps as a result of their own inner drivers and fears, sound critical, the child is likely to feel threatened, angry and unwilling to cooperate.

Of course, if the child clearly welcomes help, then the parent should feel at liberty to help or "teach" in line with the teacher's methods. As the child progresses and gains in confidence he may need less help, and as he grows into adolescence, typically becoming increasingly self-conscious and self-critical, he may prefer the parent to stay well out of way. But the odd appreciative comment: *"That was sounding lovely",* can provide much ongoing incentive, and boost confidence.

Finally, it is worth mentioning that one of the main points of practice is to give the pupil space to work out how to play for himself, without the pressure and fear of an authority figure present. So, for this reason and all those above, the parent should feel free just to concentrate on encouragement.

The "Inner Parent": "Inner Carer" or "Inner Critic"

As discussed in Chapter One, a child who has received and internalised supportive messages (from the parent teacher) easily develops an "Inner Carer" in line, and is then able to support himself internally as he practises or performs, even when the going gets tough. On the other hand, a child who has received and internalised a high proportion of critical messages, is more likely to have an "Inner Critic" that may undermine him. A critical awareness is necessary in alerting the pupil to quality and in spurring practice: if a child has no internalised critical awareness he may practise but to no effect, or perform badly without turning a hair. But there is a fine balance between inner criticism which spurs and inner criticism which destroys. Too much inner criticism can result in the pupil anxiously avoiding practice and performance.

Whatever the pupil's internal balance of Carer and Critic, though, we can't simply blame the parents (and blame wouldn't be helpful, anyway) because children play an *active*, if unconscious, role in the selection of messages they hear and internalise. Children are born different, they respond differently and they elicit different responses out of the very same parent or home environment.

Understanding Teachers and Parents

Mutual needs

Just as pupils need to feel security, success and appreciation in learning, so both parents and teachers need to feel security, success and appreciation in their roles as parents or teachers. At heart, both teachers and parents want the same thing: the happiness and progress of the child, and both teachers and parents respond to, and are motivated by, appreciation from the other.

Both are authority figures

One inherent difficulty in the teacher-parent relationship is that both parents and teachers are "authority figures". This may cause either, quite unconsciously, to key into "Inner Child" in relation to the other, and to transfer the role of "Parent" (or "Authority Figure") onto the other. *Either could then have a seemingly disproportionate need for approval and fear of disapproval from the other.* Seen from this perspective, it is then easy to understand how each may be able to threaten or slight the other, but be completely unaware of his or her capacity to do so.

Preconceived ideas

Another inherent difficulty may be that both parents and teachers may have preconceived ideas about the other's role (usually based on previous experience with other authority figures). For example, a parent may feel that the teacher "ought" to know best and that the parent "ought not" to interfere, even when the parent *knows* things are not going well. Or a teacher may feel that the parent "ought" to see that the child practises regularly and properly, "ought" to help with practice, and "ought" to make sure that he arrives for lessons on time, complete with music. Such preconceived ideas may be neither known nor shared by the other.

Establishing and Maintaining a Working Relationship

Clearly, both understanding and communication are essential in establishing and maintaining a good working relationship between parents and teachers. Such a relationship needs to be grounded not in transference or preconceived ideas, but in reality.

Opening the lines of communication

Whether we teach at home or in school it is up to us to take the initiative and open the lines of communication.

First impressions

First impressions are powerful and long-lasting. So the initial contact, whether through a website and email, text or telephone message, or in person, is very important indeed. As we know, the parent's primary need is to feel safety and security on behalf of their child. So we need to reassure them of our care, integrity and professionalism through our website, initial communication, personal appearance and the appearance of our teaching studio.

The initial consultation lesson

An initial consultation lesson, in which some time is spent with the parent, can be very helpful to find out about each other's hopes and expectations, and establish some ground rules. Commonly teachers and parents need to discuss:

- the parent's hopes and expectations for lessons
- the teacher's aims and general approach
- the teacher's initial proposals for this particular child
- lesson times, fees and procedure in the case of cancellation by teacher or pupil
- parental involvement with lessons to suit the individual teacher and parent

It may be helpful to set some or all of this out in a contract which both parent and teacher sign. Contracts protect both parties and, through prior legally binding agreement, help reduce stress when difficulties (e.g. late cancellations or non-payment of fees) occur.

Parental involvement with practice

Perhaps at the outset, but definitely as lessons progress, teachers and parents need to discuss:

> ***Where*** **the pupil should practise:** Young pupils tend to prefer to practise in a family-friendly part of the house where the instrument is invitingly open and ready. They can be put off if they are expected to go to a little used part of the house by themselves. Older pupils may prefer to practise where no one can hear. Headphones on digital pianos can be very useful for silent practice.
>
> ***When*** **to practise:** A practice timetable could be drawn up which is suited to the demands of the family's schedule, after school activities, homework, favourite TV programmes and any other commitments. Pupils at any age may need help and reminding to stick to the schedule.
>
> ***What*** **and** ***How*** **to practise:** Remembering that pupils tend to feel more motivated if *they* have decided what to practise in discussion with their teacher, and if they have memorised, or written it down (see Chapter Three), parents may be asked to read the practice agreed, and go through it with the pupil at practice time.
>
> **The parental role in practice:** Bearing in mind the psychology explained earlier, and depending on the particular dynamic between pupil and parent, we may like to explain to parents that we like them to support and encourage practice, but only to give active help if the pupil welcomes it. We can ask parents just to let us know, by email, text or telephone, where the child found difficulty, and what he avoided practising. We can also ask them to sign the practice notebook verifying that practice has been done, perhaps adding a comment. The more we know, the more we can help, and the pupil is more likely to settle down to difficulty in our professionally experienced hands.
>
> Parents can be heartened to realise that we fully understand *why* practice can be such a minefield, and *why* we don't wish, or expect, them to coerce an unwilling child.

Teaching in school

If teaching in schools we may need to make a special effort, preferably with the knowledge and support of the Head of Music, to contact parents to discuss expectations, approaches and practice and to maintain regular contact. Lessons "out of sight" are usually "out of mind" where busy parents are concerned, and there'll be an assumption that "all's well" if there's no contact from the teacher.

Teaching in the pupil's home

There are many advantages to teaching in the pupil's home. We can make sure that the home set up is as conducive to practice as possible: the instrument in good repair, the stool at the right height, the music stand readily available, the lighting adequate and the extraneous noise levels manageable etc. Also, in seeing the pupil in his own home we can get to know him more quickly, gaining in understanding and insight, and, in having regular contact with parents, we can more easily engender a mutually cooperative working relationship.

It is more usual than not to be treated with professional respect when visiting pupils' homes, but we should raise, tactfully, any issue we do not feel comfortable with. It has not been unknown for the teacher to be left not only with the pupil, but also in charge of various siblings whilst the parent goes out with the inevitable detrimental effect on lessons!

Even if, as a rule, we teach in our own home or in a school, it can be very helpful to teach at least one lesson in the pupil's home, or, perhaps, to teach once a year in the pupil's home (so long as this suggestion is welcomed by the parent) in order to check the practice set up and strengthen relations with both pupils and parents.

Dealing with Difficulty

As indicated above, most difficulties arise through misunderstanding and lack of communication between teachers and parents, and they are exacerbated by the possible transferences and pre-conceived ideas at play.

The need for regular contact

Regular contact with parents is important. We need to explain to parents that we like ongoing discussion and contact, and that we like to be kept in touch with anything affecting the child, and to nip problems in the bud. We should give our preferred contact details and ask parents how they prefer to be contacted.

The tendency to delay contact

However, there is, unfortunately, an overwhelming tendency for teachers and parents to delay contacting each other, perhaps through sheer busy-ness, perhaps through hoping the problem will go away, perhaps through not knowing how to approach the other, and through fearing what the other might think or do!

Approaching the parent

Should we need to approach the parent we should try to:

- begin by giving the parent appreciation, knowing that this is the best way to engender positive discussion
- explain ourselves clearly whilst remembering the parent may have a different point of view
- invite the parent's point of view
- listen and try to understand what the parent is really saying
- resist the urge to be defensive
- be open in discussion, remembering that a better solution than any we might previously have had in mind may arise out of the discussion
- remember that parent needs to feel secure, successful and appreciated in their role

When approaching the parent, it is best to make personal contact or speak on the telephone rather than write a letter, email or text, because the written word can so easily be misinterpreted, especially when emotions are running high. If writing is unavoidable, we need to reassure the parent of our concern and suggest that we meet to discuss the problem. In any communication, written or spoken, we should be careful not to say anything that could be interpreted as self-justifying at the expense of the parent. If the parent feels belittled, however unintentionally, the relationship will be threatened and the pupil may be removed.

When parents approach teachers

If a parent needs to approach us it is better done in the early stages of the perceived problem. Unfortunately, as explained above, parents may not approach us until late in the day when they are thoroughly exasperated, but before we have been aware of any difficulty. Out of the blue we can be faced with an irate parent:

> *"When is Mary going to take an exam?!"*

Our initial response to such an angry opener is to feel threatened. However, we need to *resist the urge to react defensively or aggressively in response* and, instead, try to identify the cause of the anger. More often than not, anger is caused by a sense of threat.

In this example, for instance, the parent may have felt threatened because she had the *preconceived idea* that all pupils took music exams as soon as they were able, and that as Mary had not yet been entered, it showed that either Mary, or the teacher, *wasn't good enough.* (A straightforward sense of threat.)

When dealing with difficulties with parents, just as when dealing with difficulties with pupils (see Chapter Four), we need to allow time and a safe space, use observation and countertransference, accept feelings, gently reflect and paraphrase feelings and ask open questions. We also need to feel secure enough in our own professional position and personal dignity to be able to listen with an open mind, understanding the parent's difficulty and entering into genuine discussion. Finally, we need to trust that the right solution, whatever that may be, will emerge, in its own time, out of the discussion. Perhaps the potentially difficult dialogue opened above could have been handled as follows:

Parent: *"When is Mary going to take an exam?!"*

It sounded aggressive and felt threatening.

Teacher: *"When is Mary going to take an exam? That's a very good question ... Have you a moment or two to discuss this?"*

Using countertransference, the teacher realised that the parent was feeling threatened. When replying she reflected the parent's feelings ("*When is Mary going to take an exam?)* both to enable the parent to feel heard, *and* to give herself time to think what to say. She also managed to give approval to encourage positive feeling *("a very good question")* and invited the parent to stay to discuss the situation properly.

Parent: *"I want her to take an exam. Isn't she good enough yet? All her friends are doing them! Some are on Grade Two!"*

When the parent heard her feelings reflected she felt they were accepted, which enabled her to open up and explain further (rather than close up in aggressive defence).

Teacher: *"Oh I see!"* realising that the parent saw exams as markers of progress and success: *"Yes, Mary could do an exam. She's up to the standard where Grade One would be realistic in a term or two. But is that what we really want for her? Exams develop some skills but not others, and I'm not sure Mary will enjoy all of the set pieces. Only a few boards offer improvisation and Mary enjoys that and is very good at it, so I would like to make sure, whatever we do, that she continues improvising.*

Supposing you let me gather all the information from the different exam boards and we have a proper talk about it all next week?"

Parent: On feeling that her wishes were being seriously considered, and realising that there's more to it than she had thought, the parent happily agreed and went away to collect her thoughts for the next week.

The following phrases may also be useful to encourage discussion and diffuse anger:

"Your interest and help make such a difference. I was wondering if you might have had any thoughts about what to do about ...."

"I was wondering if it might be possible for me to ... or for you to ... what do you think?"

"Yes, I do see your point of view."

"I hadn't realised ... that's helpful to know."

"Thank you so much ..."

And if stuck or floored:

"May I give that a week's thought?"

"May I telephone you this evening?"

Dealing with Difficulties

- **Explain that you like parents to be in touch to discuss difficulties.** Give your preferred contact details.

- **Give appreciation as often as possible.** It lays secure ground for the way ahead.

- **If feeling attacked, avoid leaping to your defence, but accept their feelings, gently repeating what you heard.** This helps them feel understood, and takes the wind out of their sails.

- **Ask questions to find out more about their point of view.** The more they feel understood, the more ready they will feel to hear your point of view.

- **Gently state your point of view, and make and invite suggestions.** Avoid being attached to being right, or to a particular outcome.

- **Trust that a mutually satisfying solution will arise out of the discussion.**

Summary and Practical Checklist

PARENTS

Pupils and Parents

- The parent's primary role is caregiving, support and encouragement.
- The parent is also experienced as the ultimate authority (life giver or annihilator). If the parent tries to "teach" the child, or otherwise criticises, suggesting the child is not good enough, the child may feel his internal support going (from both his parent and from his own inner self) resulting in a terrified temper tantrum or flat refusal.
- Parents have an important role in helping the child develop his internal support and resource, his "Inner Carer". The strength of the child's "Inner Carer" and "Inner Critic" depends not only on the parent but also on the child.
- On the whole young pupils like to have a space to practise at the hub of family life with an encouraging parent close by. Older pupils may prefer to practise in a room by themselves, with the odd appreciative and encouraging comment from parents: *"That was sounding lovely!"*

Teachers and Parents

- Both teachers and parents are authority figures which may result in each having a disproportionate need for approval and fear of disapproval from the other.
- Both teachers and parents like to feel security, success and appreciation in their roles. Giving appreciation enables the flow of positive energy.
- It is up to us to open the lines of communication remembering that the parent needs to feel in safe hands. First impressions (heightened emotional intensity) are very important. Lessons, fees, cancellation procedures and when and where to practise all need to be discussed at the outset. It may be useful to draw up a contract.
- As a general rule, but depending on the particular dynamic pupil and parent, we may like to ask the parent only to encourage the pupil during practice but to report back to us if the pupil has experienced difficulty and/or avoided practice. It may be helpful to explain the underlying psychology.
- We may need to be very clear that we welcome feedback and ongoing discussion remembering that there is an overwhelming tendency to delay contact.
- If the pupil learns at school, we may need to make a special effort to contact and stay in touch with parents.
- If the pupil does not learn in his house it may be helpful for us to teach at least once (perhaps once a year?) in the pupil's house. In this way our relationship with the parent can be strengthened, we can gain insight into the child and the home set-up can be helpfully checked out.
- In discussion with parents we need to allow time and a safe space, use countertransference, accept feelings, gently reflect and paraphrase feelings and ask open questions. We need to feel secure enough in ourselves to listen with an open mind, understanding the parent's difficulty, refusing to feel threatened, avoiding putting the parent on the defensive and entering into genuine discussion. We need to trust that the right solution will emerge in its own time out of the discussion.

Personal Reflection

PARENTS

Reflect briefly on the contents of the chapter. Make a note of the points of particular interest to you below. Then, compile your personal practical checklist on the following page.

Finally, visualise yourself putting any new ideas from your checklist into practice.

Personal Practical Checklist

PARENTS

Chapter Eight: Age-Related Learning Guide

Summary of Chapters One to Seven

"The Golden Rule is that there are no golden rules"

Anonymous

Although there are no hard and fast rules, these things depending on individual nature and nurture, as a general guide:

Pupils Aged 4-10

- Need warmth, encouragement and appreciation from the teacher
- Need to play tunes they know and tunes they like
- Learn by listening and doing rather than thinking
- Need to be taken step-by-step through note reading, counting and clapping, learning note names, assimilating shapes and patterns (e.g. up, down, space to space, line to line)
- Need to have plenty of easy material to read and play
- Need to have tasks "contained" or "framed" into easily digestible, bite-sized pieces
- Respond to metaphor and imagery
- Respond unselfconsciously to internalising musical elements through the body
- Prefer more teacher than pupil-direction
- May like parents to be present to support and encourage (only) at practice time
- Like to improvise, perhaps on a theme: The Park, Going to Bed, The School Playground, or perhaps making musical illustrations to poems and stories
- Like to use graphic notation
- Like individual lessons and group lessons
- Like to make music NOW

Pupils Aged 11-18

- Need warmth, encouragement, appreciation, approval and reassurance from the teacher
- Respond to being encouraged to decide what to learn from a variety of musical styles and skills to ensure they are pursuing their own interests (not necessarily standard syllabi)
- There may be a greater tendency to learn by understanding, then doing, rather than simply learning by doing
- Need to have tasks "contained" or "framed" into easily digestible, bite-sized pieces
- Respond to metaphor and imagery
- Depending on previous experience (or lack of it), they may feel less comfortable internalising musical elements through the body than younger pupils

- Prefer a mixture of teacher and pupil-direction
- As music reading skills increase, they may feel increasingly able to learn and practise by themselves, only requiring step-by-step guidance from the teacher on the "difficult bits"
- May be interested in improvisation, but may need help because they feel worried about "getting it wrong" and "not making nice sounds"
- May like people to stay well out of the way when they are practising, but the odd appreciative comment, especially from parents, can be very motivating
- May like to compose using graphic notation
- Like individual lessons and mutually supportive group lessons
- Like to make music NOW

Adult Pupils

- May suffer acutely from keying back into infantile emotions, yet knowing this seems ridiculous, worrying unduly what the teacher might be thinking about them, yet knowing this is absurd, and trying to hide all of these feelings(!) but needing the teacher to understand and help them into the adult part of themselves
- Need warmth, encouragement, appreciation, reassurance and understanding from the teacher
- Need adult sounding music as soon as possible, suitable, tasteful arrangements of much- loved music can be very motivating
- Probably quick in terms of intellectual understanding, and likely to feel "safer" with the written music owing to years of school and office work with eye-intellect rather than ear-finger coordination
- Aural skills variable depending upon earlier musical training
- Likely to feel frustrated with fingers
- Need to have tasks "contained" or "framed" into easily digestible, bite-sized pieces
- Respond to metaphor and imagery
- May respond to internalising musical elements through bodily movement, but may through lack of early experience find it daunting and difficult
- Probably prefer to direct their own lessons in consultation with the teacher (they know why they want to learn and what they want to achieve), but there remains a sense in which the teacher "knows best" and should be allowed to guide and suggest, particularly in helping the pupil learn how to do it
- May need help sorting out a practice timetable to fit in with work and family commitments
- May enjoy improvisation, for example, on pentatonic or modal scales over held open fifth or sixth chords; on major or minor scales over the primary chords, or experimenting with chordal progressions; and on jazz scales over the twelve bar blues
- Like individual lessons and may like mutually supportive group lessons
- Like to make music NOW

Personal Reflection

AGE-RELATED LEARNING GUIDE

Summary of Chapters One to Seven

Reflect briefly on the contents of the chapter. Make a note of the points of particular interest to you below. Then, compile your personal practical checklist on the following page.

Finally, visualise yourself putting any new ideas from your checklist into practice.

Personal Practical Checklist

AGE-RELATED LEARNING GUIDE

Summary of Chapters One to Seven

Chapter Nine: Performance

Anxiety, Communication and Safety

"We all have inner judges who yammer at the edge of our consciousness, often intimidating and immobilising us. We can look these judges squarely in the face, and learn to deal with them in ways that free us of their tyranny. We may even change them from monitoring, censuring critics into common-sense allies and supporting figures."

Eloise Ristad, A Soprano on Her Head, 1982

EXERCISE: EXPLORING PERFORMING

Using the bubbles below (adding more if you need), recall and write down your feelings and thoughts during your own performance, when it's going well:

Examples that come up regularly in doing this exercise:

Enjoying being here, enjoying being part of a group, enjoying the challenge, enjoying letting go, enjoying giving pleasure, loving the music.

Feeling excitement, delight, interest, surprise, exhilaration, pride, a sense of achievement.

Feeling it's okay to make a mistake, several mistakes, it's even relaxing to make a mistake.

Saying helpful things internally: "Keep steady, don't rush"; "Listen to the acoustic".

Feeling warm audience response, feeling the audience are totally there with me;

Realising in retrospect that when "in flow" nothing much, and especially nothing disturbing, frightening or awkward passes through feelings or thoughts.

Now recall and write down your feelings and thoughts during your own performance, first, when it threatens to go wrong, then, when it *is* going wrong (add more bubbles if you need):

Examples:

Being aware of physical discomfort: shaking, stiffness, tension, respiration and heartbeat going haywire.

Fearing letting the soloist or group down, fearing not knowing the music well enough, fearing a memory lapse, not daring to feel, not daring to let go and take risks, fear of looking a complete fool.

Striving for perfection, giving myself a hard time: "Why do I do this to myself?"

Worrying about who is there and what they think: "Who does she think she is?" "What on earth is he doing on stage?" "She can't play at all!" "He's useless!"

Feeling heart sink, disappointment, frustration, annoyance, terror, boredom.

Not being fully present, wishing it was all over, wishing I was somewhere else, wishing the floor would open up and swallow me whole.

Feeling I'm falling apart, dying of shame.

EXERCISE: EXPLORING AUDIENCES

Now think and write down what you would like from the performers and the performance when you are in the audience:

Typical responses are:

To be engaged, connected with, uplifted, excited, delighted, inspired, entertained, transported, feeling soul communication, outpouring of spirit.

Wanting the performers to succeed, to be in charge so that I feel safe, comfortable and can relax. Not wanting to feel the musicians need to be supported or picked up.

If the performance you are listening to begins to get a little ragged and then threatens to fall apart altogether, what are your initial and subsequent responses?

Typical responses are:

Initially I wonder whether something's happened. Did I miss something?

I might start switching off a little, my attention might wander.

I start thinking about things I have to do when I get home.

I will them on, wanting them to succeed.

If they look nervous and embarrassed I feel uncomfortable and embarrassed for them.

If they look extremely uncomfortable I wish I was somewhere else.

Did you notice any difference in your attitude to *yourself* when you are performing and your attitude to *others* when they are performing (when you are in the audience)? Especially, did you notice any difference in your attitude towards yourself and others, when things threaten to go wrong, or are going wrong?

Consider your answers in terms of understanding performing and performance anxiety, understanding what audiences want from performers, and how best to prepare yourself and your pupils for performing.

Understanding Performing

Performing is the live communication of music. We go to performances to be immersed in music, to relax and enjoy it. We perform because we love music, we love making music and we want to express that music, to share it with others. Usually, we choose a programme with interest and enjoyment, practice with diligence and enjoyment, feeling a sense of purpose in our work, and look forward to the occasion with a keen sense of anticipation and enjoyment. But how much do we actually *enjoy the occasion?* All of it all of the time? Most of it, most of the time? Sometimes? Or only afterwards when it's over?

Understanding Performance Anxiety

For most of us, the actual occasion produces at least some, if not a great deal, of anxiety. We find ourselves in a state of fear whereby, from a physiological perspective, we freeze with *"fright"*, but experience a rush of adrenalin which goes to the vital organs to prepare us for *"flight"* or *"fight"*. Helpful as this may have been for our ancestors when fleeing from or fighting against dangers, it can be profoundly unhelpful for us, as it results in:

- difficulty with respiration and an overactive pulse
- loss of fine motor control: our fingers feel as though they no longer belong to us
- an inability to think clearly: we "go stupid"
- emotional and expressive constriction

Keying into "Inner Child"

From a psychological perspective, performance anxiety can cause us to key into "Inner Child". In "Inner Child" we then cast the audience or examiner into the role of "Parent" (or "Authority Figure"), having a seemingly out of proportion need for their approval and fear of their criticism. It can feel as though our very life depends upon their reception of us.

Like the helpless infant, we feel as though we're falling apart, or just about to fall into the bottomless pit that's suddenly opened up within us. We can spend the whole performance wishing that we were somewhere else, or that it was all over.

Understanding What the Audience and Examiners Want

It is through being in touch with what we want from performers when we are in the audience that we can make conscious and healthy decisions about how to be as performers.

Ironically, in view of our needs when in "Inner Child", it is the *audience* who wants to feel safe in *our* hands, who wants *us* to take charge, and not to allow any slips to adversely affect the music, or ourselves. It is only if they feel safe that they can relax, open up and respond to the music. Examiners, too, *want* to enjoy the music, and they want to feel that they have given the candidate the right result. They can more readily feel that their decision to pass the candidate is the right one if the candidate is clearly in charge of himself, in charge of his performance and in charge of the situation, *whatever happens during the performance.*

The Performer is the Person in Charge

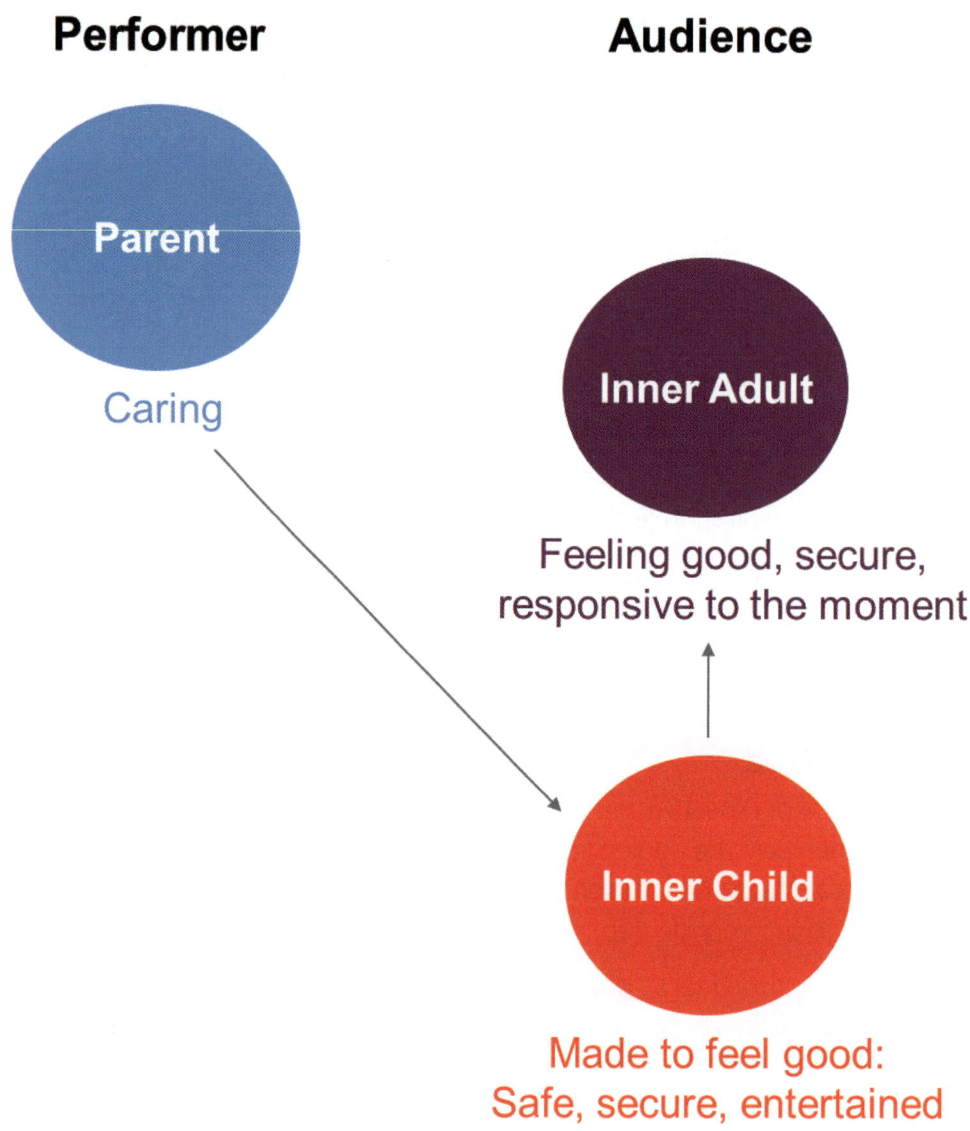

Audiences *want* performers to take the role of ***Parent***, being in charge *whatever* happens during the performance, then they can relax and enjoy it.

Unhelpful Societal Notions: "Show off!" "Who do you think you are?"

Arguably, it is primarily the notions we pick up from our society that can make it difficult for us to feel in charge and enjoy performing.

A commonly held notion in our society is that it's not okay to perform, much less to *enjoy* performing. In childhood, our naturally expressive spirits may have been crushed with put-downs such as: *"Show off!"* or: *"Who do you think you are?"* These sort of notions can even be found in our nursery rhyme games: an exuberant: *"I'm the king of the castle!"* is met with the sharp retort: *"Get down you dirty rascal!"*

Such repression of early expression leads us to feel that it's not safe or right to express our feelings, so we learn to repress them and, in doing so, we gradually lose touch with them. Then, having lost touch with our own feelings, far from being able to play from our own inner authority, we find ourselves playing to please or appease others, playing to give them what we *think* they want, hoping that it will go all right, and fearing that it won't.

Following on from this, another unhelpful societal notion is that thinking and left-brained quantitive skills, such as logic, analysis and dissection, are rated higher than feeling and right-brained qualitative skills, such as intuition and artistic expression. (As evidence of this we need look no further than the average pay packets of lawyers and accountants versus musicians and artists). This may result in our believing that being note perfect (a quantitive and measurable thing) is more important than being expressive and making satisfying musical connections (qualitative, subjective things). Finally, our society is hierarchical, "top-dog, under-dog". Competition is evident everywhere and appears to be rated more highly than cooperation or mutual support. This may result in our feeling that unless we are the best, or one of the best, it's not worth performing, or it's wrong to perform *("Show off!")*, or it's simply inviting criticism to perform at all.

The "Inner Parent": "Inner Critic" or "Inner Carer"

Exposure to any societal notions, including the ones described above, results in our *internalising* them, so that they become part of our "Inner Parent", whether predominantly critical (the "Inner Critic") or caring (the "Inner Carer").

The "Inner Critic"

As evident from the above, the internalisation of our particular societal notions is likely to result in a strong "Inner Critic" who says inside our heads, for example: *"I'm nothing unless I'm the best", or: "I'm nothing unless I'm perfect", or: "It's only if I play perfectly that I'm safe from critical attack"*. No wonder performing is such an ordeal for so many of us!

We also need to be aware that whatever the strength of our personal "Inner Critic" (and this depends not only on our society but also on our parenting, our teachers and our innate dispositions, see Chapter One), we unconsciously "project" it out onto the audience or examiners, feeling sure that *they* will be similarly critical. So those of us with a strong "Inner Critic" will feel sure that the audience or examiners will be strongly critical, perhaps even to the extent of *wanting* to catch us out, criticise and destroy us. Whereas those with a less strong "Inner Critic" will feel more relaxed.

A strong "Inner Critic" is also likely to make us very critical of others, perhaps because we feel, unconsciously: *"I'm given a hard time so I'll give others a hard time too"*, or perhaps because we simply don't know how else to be. It can also be the driving pressure of a strong "Inner Critic" which makes us take perverse pleasure in someone else's misfortune: *"Phew! He made lots of mistakes, I know I can play better than that. At least I won't be the worst!"* But, even with a strong "Inner Critic", we tend to give others far more support when they are performing than we give ourselves when we perform.

Whatever our critical disposition towards ourselves and others, it can be helpful to our performances to foster our "Inner Carer", the caring, supportive, appreciative and encouraging self.

The "Inner Carer"

With a strong "Inner Carer" *("Go David, Go David!"),* we can feel certain, through our own "projections", that audiences and examiners *are* appreciative and encouraging. A strong "Inner Carer" is also helpful because we only have our inner selves to fall back on if things start to go wrong during performance: *"Whoopsadaisy! Never mind!"* or: *"I'm not letting this get in my way, I'm not going to go wobbly"* (the "Inner Carer") can be of much more use to the situation than: *"They must be thinking you're useless"* (the "Inner Critic").

Gender Differences

To generalise, and of course there are exceptions, it is particularly girls and women who need a strong "Inner Carer" as they need to feel safe and approved of *before* they feel free to express, therefore expose, themselves. A typical feminine feeling is: *"If I really lay bare my soul the audience will see who I really am, and they might reject the real me. It's better not to show the real me until and unless I feel totally safe, totally approved of and unconditionally accepted".*

Boys and men, on the other hand, perhaps seeing performance more in terms of *doing* than *being,* tend to *expect* to go out and prove themselves, feeling that *that* is the way to gain the approval and admiration they seek.

Balancing the "Inner Carer and "Inner Critic"

Although a strong "Inner Critic" is not always helpful, it would be a mistake to think there is no place for an "Inner Critic" at all. A critical *awareness* is necessary in alerting us to quality and in spurring work (as explained in Chapter One), it is simply that too much criticism can destroy both ourselves and our pupils.

Whatever the balance of "Inner Critic" and "Inner Carer", and the ideal balance is whatever best motivates the individual in performance (perhaps warm self-support surrounding a critically aware appreciation), it can also be helpful to draw on the "Free Inner Child".

The "Free Inner Child"

Per form ing literally means "through do ing", or "doing it now". To "do it now" we need to key into the "Free Inner Child".

The "Free Inner Child" neither seeks approval nor fears disapproval, but lives totally centred in the present moment and responds to it spontaneously. In the same way, we need neither seek the audience's or examiners' approval nor fear their disapproval, we need neither try to recreate the way we played at the last performance, nor wish we were somewhere else nor wish it was all over. Rather, we need to concentrate on being fully centred in the present moment, playing in spontaneous response to how we feel *now.* It is in our present moment engagement that we become engaging, so that the audience (or examiner) cannot help but be caught up in our engagement and engage too (countertransference, see Chapter Four).

Connecting with the "Deep Self" and with the Audience

Through being fully centred in the present moment, playing in response to now, we can also play from a deeply centred sense of self, connecting with the solar plexus, the nerve centre in our belly, that place of *inner authority,* the "Deep Self". Not only is this where music is best played from, but playing from here enables us to be fully balanced and centred in our whole body, in control of our muscles and away from any distracting, critical chatter in our heads. We can then make beautiful music, with warm and loving intention from the depths of our inner selves through our instrument out into the room and back again, so that it feels good and sounds good and so that we are enjoying it. It is *only* if we are enjoying it that the audience can enjoy it too (countertransference again), and it is in their enjoyment, or "enjoinment", as we *feel* their responsiveness, that our playing is deepened and enriched. We *find* ourselves responding spontaneously to the audience, perhaps shaping a phrase in a way that we never have before, or perhaps taking extraordinary risks, or playing with extra panache, zest and sparkle, keeping them on the edge of their seats in a way that we didn't know we could!

Positive Energy

Just as in a lesson where there is a mutual exchange of positive energy between teacher and pupil, there is a feeling of creation in action, so, in a performance where there is a mutual exchange of positive energy between performer and audience, the new, thrilling and unforgettable happens. In both cases it is a result of an "Adult" to "Adult" rather than a "Child" to "Parent" relationship. But it takes both emotional resource, practical know how and emotional, physical and mental preparation.

A typical good performance

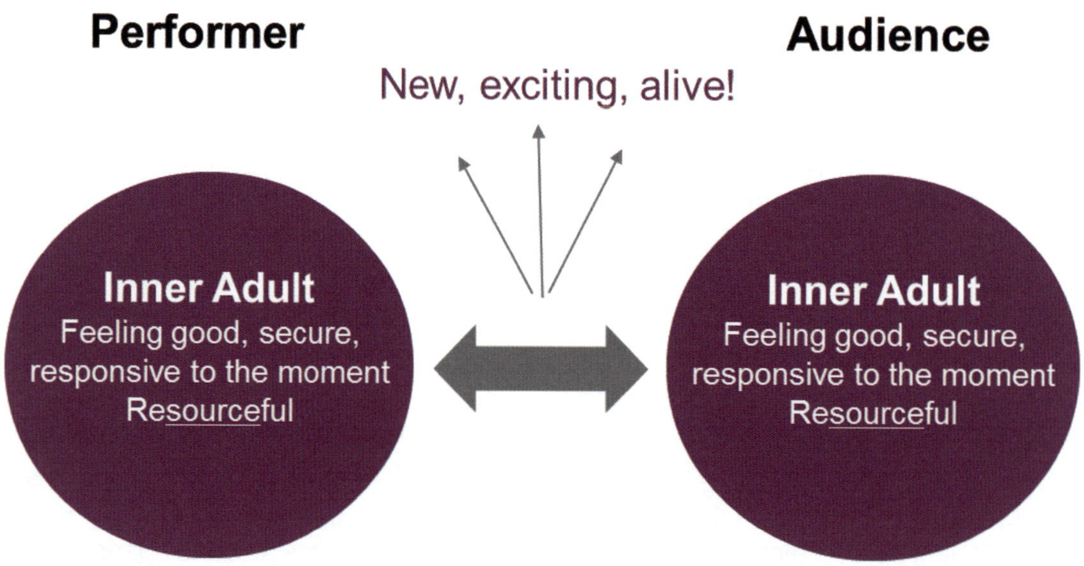

Both performer and audience are feeling secure, comfortable and engaged with the performance. There is an energetic connection between performer and audience which makes the performance feel new in the moment, exciting and alive.

Practical Suggestions for Preparation for Performance:

Emotional, Physical and Mental

On the following pages there are many practical suggestions for emotional, physical and mental preparation for performance. There is then a page specifically on what to do just before performing, and a final page giving suggestions on how to enjoy performing itself. All of the suggestions are designed to enable performers to play with inner authority, combating anxiety, enhancing and enriching musical communication, and feeling technical security and safety in performance.

Emotional Preparation for Performance

To combat the "Inner Critic", strengthen the "Inner Carer" and connect, through the "Free Inner Child" with the "Deep Self" and the audience:

- **Be in charge:** As you practice, notice where *you* feel aurally and mentally clear and physically secure, connected and comfortable. Then work to increase that sense of secure, connected comfort throughout the piece. (If you do this with your pupils, you may need to emphasise that the pupil is to connect with what *he* feels and thinks, rather than with what he thinks *you* think.)
- **Concentrate on making your playing feel and sound enjoyable *for you*:** Only if you are enjoying it can the audience or examiner enjoy it as, through countertransference (see Chapter Four), they can feel everything that you feel.
- **Play from the warmth of your solar plexus, the "Deep Self":** Connect with your deep inner self and play from there, listening to the sound as it goes out through your instrument into the corners of the room and back to you.
- **Be aware:** When you slip up, go back and tackle the section thoroughly. Listen to your fears, they will be telling you what is still not secure. Don't hide from yourself.
- **Play with playing:** Make spontaneous expression, rather than getting the notes right, the priority. For example:

  deliberately intensify nerves and *try* to make mistakes (not so easy, is it?!)

  see how relaxed you can be, and still play

  play too fast or too slow

  play a tragic piece playfully, a jolly piece mournfully etc.

  dare to experiment, express any inner musical feeling as it arises

  You can only know *how* much by trying *too* much.
- **Imagine being the audience or the examiner:** Think what you would like and what your priorities would be. Presumably you would like to be caught up in the performance, you wouldn't want to see the performer being upset by any error, and you would want him to succeed. It is only if he is enjoying himself that you could fully enjoy yourself.

- **Practice Performing in a Safe Circle:** Gather a group of players (colleagues or pupils) who want to practise performing in a supportive environment. Tell them that they are only allowed to feel and think positive and appreciative things about the performance in progress. (This is especially useful in developing the listeners' "Inner Carers" for them to draw on when they perform later).

  Everyone performs in turn, and at the end of each performance each member of the group says something he enjoyed about the performance to the performer, beginning: *"I loved ...", "I enjoyed ..."* Or: *"I appreciated ..."* from a position of equals rather than from a position of judgement. The performer then says what he enjoyed performing and what parts he wants to work on.

- **Play the *"And Then"* game:** Explore your worst possible fears about performance with a colleague or friend who listens carefully but responds only by saying *"And then?"* until a natural conclusion is reached. For example:

Performer:	*"I go onto the platform to play, I sit down, look at the keyboard ... and I can't remember what on earth the first notes are!"*
Colleague:	*"And then ..."*
Performer:	*"I do remember, just about, and start."*
Colleague:	*"And then ..."*
Performer:	*"It's okay, I settle in for a bit'... "*
Colleague:	*"And then ..."*
Performer:	*"I've not really settled, I'm getting less rather than more sure ... and I know I'm just about to seize up "*
Colleague:	*"And then ..."*
Performer:	*"Help! I stop altogether!"*
Colleague:	*"And then ..."*
Performer:	*"I start fumbling for some notes and play anything I can remember and feel really awful. I can tell the audience are feeling sorry for me and distancing themselves and thinking I'm useless ... "*
Colleague:	*"And then ..."*
Performer:	*"I can't even remember the key or the last chord ... I want the floor to open up and swallow me up."*
Colleague:	*"And then ..."*
Performer:	*"I run away off stage."*
Colleague:	*"And then ..."*
Performer:	*"I cry into my teacher's arms ... "*
Colleague:	*"And then ..."*
Performer:	*"I never, ever do it again."*
Colleague:	*"And then ..."*

Performer: *"Maybe one day much, much later I have another go, but maybe not from memory, or maybe learning specific start points, maybe with other musicians not by myself. I still want to play music."*

Colleague: *"And then ... "*

Performer: *"Then I feel better, doing it for me on my terms ... "*

The performer has now reached an inner resolution. He has become conscious of his worst fears and begun to develop a strategy to deal with them (*"maybe not from memory, or maybe learning specific start points").*

Very often this exercise enables performers to see the absurdity, the irrationality and, simply, the funny side of their fears. As humour is such a vitalising and releasing force this exercise is often excellent to do, in a light-hearted manner, just before performing.

- Dialogue with the "Inner Critic": Place two chairs (or cushions) opposite each other. Sit in one and, from there, talk to the other seat, where your "Inner Critic" is "sitting". Then, when ready, move to that seat to "become" your "Inner Critic" and reply to yourself. This process is known as "Hot seating" and often leads to insights. For example:

Performer: addressing an empty seat or cushion opposite him:
"Why do you expect me to be so perfect all the time?"
The Performer now moves to the empty seat or cushion to become the "Inner Critic" and responds back to the Performer:

Inner Critic: *"Because I know you can do it!"*

Performer: (continuing to move from seat to seat for each impersonation):
"But it puts huge pressure on me. I feel as though I'm not acceptable if I can't do it."

Inner Critic: *"You are acceptable just the way you are. But you want to produce a perfectly exquisite piece of art if you can, don't you?"*

Performer: *"Yes! But it might not come out right on the day, and you'll give me a very hard time and make me feel I'm not acceptable."*

Inner Critic: *"I'm sorry, maybe that's unreasonably hard, I didn't know you felt so bad about that. How would you like to feel?"*

Performer: *"I'd like to feel warmth and mutual acceptance however it comes on the night, because all I want is for a musical connection between me and the audience which is mutually enriching. I don't care about perfection. Just contact."*

Inner Critic: *"Oh! I see."*

Performer: *"So your perfectionist demands are useless because they make me self-conscious and inwardly critical and make me wonder what the audience are thinking, instead of making me reach out in warmth to the audience!!! Do you see?!!"*

Inner Critic: *"You've made me feel rather small now. I can see I haven't been what you've wanted or needed."*

Performer: (crying) *"And you've given me a heck of a lot of distress!! Plain perfection is no good! Its communication that matters! And you can communicate just by being you ... without any notes!"*

The performer now feels finished. He has reached a clearer understanding of how his "Inner Critic" impeded his musical expression and has inwardly resolved to focus on practising for *expression* rather than for his old idea of *"perfection"*.

Physical and Mental Preparation for Performance:

Aural, kinaesthetic and intellectual/visual skills

In order to feel secure in performance (and able to function even in the throes of any performance anxiety) aural, kinaesthetic (physical) and intellectual/visual (mental) skills are all necessary. We need to know not only the *sound* of every note we play (melodies, countermelodies and harmonies), but also the *feel* of playing every note and the *look* of every note both on the page and on the instrument.

A good question to keep asking yourself as you practise is: *"What am I feeling in my body, where do I need to feel more comfortable as I play?"* The more comfortable the physical movement, the more easily the piece will be learnt. Sensibly, muscles resist learning anything uncomfortable because they know it may result in injury. Forcing your body against its own comfort will result in injury or impairment.

Clear mental representation of the music you are playing and how you are playing it (including fingering) is also essential. You need to concentrate.

Listening, and being fully physically and mentally conscious practise:

- Slowly, at a speed at which you *can't* make mistakes, rhythmically, firmly and warmly relish every note with ears, fingers, eyes and intellect so that it sinks in very deeply feeling warm, connected and physically secure. It can be helpful to imagine that your fingers are sinking into velvet cushions, kneading dough or deeply massaging the instrument.
- Hands separately, with and without sound on a digital piano with the sound switched off, on the piano lid, without bowing, without blowing etc., so that the kinaesthetic aspect is reinforced and the left and the right brain have a chance to disentangle and become very clear. On wind instruments, and any other instrument where playing hands separately produces an unacceptable sound, practice only *without* sound.
- Hands together, with and without sound being aware of which finger (or arm movement) in the left goes with which finger (or arm movement) in the right, remembering that the body feels most comfortable when both left and right are doing exactly the same thing in mirror image. When left and right are doing different things (different fingers, arm movements, intervals, directions, dynamics etc.) and making slips, it may be necessary to be consciously aware of exactly what is happening. For example: the left hand moves up three notes using the 5th finger and then the 2nd, while the right moves down five notes using the 3rd finger (while left uses 5th), followed by the thumb (while left uses the 2nd).
- Fingering and saying the note names, and fingering and counting (without blowing on wind instruments and with and without sound on other instruments) helps strengthen the mental picture of the notes being played and is particularly effective in clarifying any tricky passages or difficult chords.

- **Using distorted rhythm** where  becomes , and  becomes , clearly accenting the strong beat(s) of the bar. This helps the body know where to relax (the stronger, longer beats) and where to push through, thus aiding physical comfort and muscle memory, and eliminating the stiffness so often associated with long passage playing.

Especially if performing from memory:

- **Analyse the written music** to understand the overall architecture, the form, the main themes, the variations to the main themes, phrase shapes and lengths, rhythmic and melodic patterns and chord sequences etc.
- **Practice from memory looking at the instrument (if possible)** being aware of the keys and fingering patterns. Do this hands separately (if possible on the instrument) and, when secure, do this while singing the sound the other hand makes (if possible on the instrument). Also, practise hands together from memory.
- **Divide the music into sections (of 8 bars? or 16 bars?) as musically appropriate and make sure you can begin from each of these sections from memory** so that if you have a memory slip you always have a "pick-up" point a few bars ahead or a few bars back.
- **Practise the pick-up points, hands separately and together, with and without sound.**
- **Visualise playing the notes away from the instrument, section by section,** hands separately (if possible and appropriate) and hands together, inwardly feeling the accompanying physical sensation and inwardly hearing the sound. Do this first from the written music and then (if performing from memory) without the music. Visualise in this way until you can do it in fully centred confidence and enjoyment, loving every note.
- **Practise performing** to colleagues, students, pupils, friends or family for at least two months before the performance (from memory if the performance will be from memory). Performances need to be practised both so that you gain confidence in performing, and so that you become aware of any insecurities which may not have shown up at home or in the usual lesson, with enough time still to make them secure.
- **Constantly maintain and update your repertoire:** Make sure you can always play something *now* without the music (a variety of pieces, some exciting, some short and simple). In this way you will play more often, enhance your own self-respect as a player and enjoy being a musician.

Just Before the Performance

- **Breathe deeply and rhythmically from the diaphragm:** If you hyperventilate don't do this but breathe into a paper bag for a short time. This reduces the oxygen intake and so calms you down.
- **Move:** Moving enables you to inhabit your whole body, become fully centred in it and so be fully present in the moment. It also enables you to relax, so jog gently, touch your toes, swing your arms, do cross-lateral movements, stretch and flex your muscles in any way you choose.
- **Make sure your hands are the right temperature:** If necessary immerse them in warming or cooling water.
- **Especially if you are feeling nervous, "meet" your own feeling:** Tell yourself or someone else how you feel. This helps you get in touch with yourself and enables you to centre yourself even in your nervousness.
- **Play the *"And Then"* game in a light hearted manner:** Release undue fear and engender wholesome humour. (See Emotional Preparation).
- **Use some keywords to help focus your mind and steady your concentration:** Use whichever words are most helpful to you, for example: Warmth, beauty, concentrate, enjoy.
- **Visualise yourself playing the opening of your pieces:** Can you see which notes your fingers play? Can you feel yourself producing a gorgeous tone?
- **Imagine being the audience or the examiner:** Think what you would like and what your priorities would be.
- **Centre yourself so that you can play from the warmth of your solar plexus, the nerve centre in your belly, the "Deep Self":** Sit comfortably with a straight spine and feet firmly planted on the floor. Imagine that you are slightly above your head and want to connect fully with your solar plexus and so more easily connect with your musical expression. (If you are nervous the chances are you will feel "all over the place" and too high up in your body)

  Allow yourself ten counts (from ten down to one) to collect yourself and gradually lower your consciousness through your crown, behind your eyes, nose, mouth, upper neck, collar bones, chest, lower ribs, upper stomach and into your belly and loins. Enjoy being there, and stay there, in emotional richness, and in balance with your mental awareness, as you play.

Enjoying Performing

- Be in charge and stay in charge whatever happens: The audience *wants* you to.
- Tune in to yourself: "Meet" your feeling. Tune in to the audience: "Meet" their feeling. Take your time. Walk firmly and steadily. Elicit their positive energy by your warm smile. Be fully present and responsive to the moment, spontaneous.
- Settle down into a deep place inside yourself *before* you start playing.
- Concentrate on making your playing/acting/dancing feel and sound enjoyable *for you:* Only if you are enjoying it can the audience/examiner enjoy it as, through *countertransference,* they can feel everything that you feel.
- Remember that the purpose is satisfying, expressive connection and enjoyment: Be fully connected with what you are conveying. Mistakes are irrelevant (except in rehearsal where they need full awareness and attention!).
- Play from the warmth of your solar plexus, the "Deep Self", and trust the "Deep Self": If the learning has been fully conscious, aware and clear at every level, aural, visual, intellectual and physical, it will have sunk in deeply and be easily retrieved when needed.

Secure performances happen when they are:

- **Deeply felt musically**
  - right-brained, aural and imaginative
- **Clearly and consciously known**
  - left-brained, visual and intellectual
- **Completely comfortable physically**
  - whole-brained, kinaesthetic

Personal Reflection

PERFORMANCE

Anxiety, Communication and Safety

Reflect briefly on the contents of the chapter. Make a note of the points of particular interest to you. Then, compile your personal practical checklist on the following page.

Finally, visualise yourself putting any new ideas from your checklist into practice.

Personal Practical Checklist

PERFORMANCE

Anxiety, Communication and Safety

Chapter Ten: Action Research

"The only kind of educational research that will ever actually improve education is the research done by teachers in their own classrooms to solve what they see as their own problems."

John Holt, How Children Fail, 1965

Understanding Action Research

Action research is research you do on your own teaching. The point of it is to enable you to look at any aspect of your own teaching that interests you, with the overall aim of enhancing and enriching your awareness and skills. There are seven steps which are listed below and enlarged on, where necessary, during the chapter:

- Choose a Topic
- Select your Pupils
- Define your Aims
- Design the Method
- Do the research
- Write up your Results
- Draw your Conclusions and make Recommendations for further study

There is an example of a plan for action research using these steps at the end of the chapter.

Choose a Topic

You may already know which aspect of your teaching you would like to research. If not, the twelve topics below, based on the main points of the book, may help you decide. You may like to explore one or more:

The quality of feeling or energy in lessons

What messages are you picking up about the pupil through the way you feel in the lesson? What evidence is there of the pupil's uncertainty or fear in his learning? Or his fear of you, the authority figure? (Consider any avoidance or evasion of lessons or practice). Are you tracking feelings and inspiring, "containing" feeling or shifting activity as necessary? What could you do to enhance the quality of energy in lessons?

Personal presentation and teaching environment

What sort of "parent" (Caregiving/Authoritative/Democratic) are you? Is this appropriate for the pupil in question? What transferences is the pupil making onto you? What sort of "home" is your studio? What messages is the pupil picking up through you and your studio about the whole world of music and his welcome in it and ability to be part of it? What could you do to enhance your personal presentation and teaching environment?

Praise and criticism

Is the pupil sure you value his efforts? Are you expressing praise whenever you feel it? (It is only too easy to forget to praise in the "busy-ness" of teaching). Are you teaching positively e.g. *"Those notes were phrased perfectly. Now apply that to make a longer phrase from there to there".* Sometimes criticism may be necessary to shock a pupil into action, but this only works if the pupil believes he can succeed and if the teacher-pupil relationship is strong enough so that the pupil *wants* to work to regain the temporarily lost approval. Otherwise he will give up. What could you do to enhance the effectiveness of your praise and criticism?

Learning skills

What are your pupil's predominant learning skills? Right or Left-Brained? Aural? Kinaesthetic? Intellectual/Visual? Are you using enough different teaching skills and strategies so that the pupil's strengths and weaknesses are being developed at appropriately different levels? What could you do to enhance his learning?

Teaching styles

Are lessons predominantly teacher or pupil-directed? Would the pupil benefit from more clearly defined teacher-direction (having more instruction and demonstration)? Or would he prefer more pupil-direction (having more space and freedom to tackle his own difficulties in his own way)? Would Role Reversal be helpful for the pupil? How could you employ teaching styles more effectively?

Motivation

Is the pupil learning what he feels most interested in learning as opposed to what you or others think he ought to learn? Does he know what there is on offer (in addition to standard syllabi: light/pop music, jazz, improvisation?) Is there sufficient incentive? (Informal music making with other pupils? Concerts? Exams?). What could you do to motivate him?

Practice

Is the pupil practising regularly? If not, why not? What could you do to encourage both more practice and more effective practice?

Problem pupils

Individual case studies. Which individual pupils would you like to study?

Making music now

Is the pupil able to make music now, spontaneously? Do you play together, improvise and/ or compose? Do you have fun? Could you make music more often? And could you make it more enjoyable?

Group teaching

What group teaching skills could you develop?

Parents

What could you do to strengthen the working relationship with parents?

Performance

Does the pupil feel enjoyment, physical security, mental clarity and musical connection during performance? What could you do to help him enhance his performance?

Select your Pupils

Perhaps three pupils who differ in age, ability and rapport with you (perhaps one aged 4-10, one aged 11-18 and one aged 19+). Or you may like to make a special study of one pupil? Or a group lesson?

Define your Aims

Within the area of your selected topic your aims may include:

- increased awareness and understanding of your pupils and their processes
- increased awareness and understanding of your teaching and its effects on your pupils
- increase in skills for your pupils
- increase in skills for you in your teaching

Be specific about exactly what you are hoping for.

Design your Method

Decide on the period of time for the research (at least three but no more than ten weeks of lessons). Use the four research methods below and any additional ones of your own choosing.

Observation of your teaching on video

Video the selected pupils' first and final lessons during the action research. Use a stand or tripod so no one else need be present.

While watching the replay of the first lessons, you can gain an objective sense of the quality of feeling or energies present and you will find yourself remembering how you were feeling and what was going through your head at the time. You can then see how your internal processes affected your external behaviour, which may be quite surprising. Many a teacher has been surprised and enlightened by, for example, realising that when she feels anxious or pressured she appears overbearing, or when she feels helpless she appears uncaring, and so on. As your awareness increases throughout the research, the video of the final lesson is very likely to show an increase in sensitivity in relation to your pupils.

Self-awareness

Observe your internal processes, your feelings and your thoughts as you teach. Keep a note book handy to jot them down as they occur so you can reflect on them later. Notice how your feelings and thoughts change according to different pupils and different situations. Be particularly aware of:

- Your feeling as an indicator of the pupil's feeling (countertransference).

- What is said inside your head as you teach, as an indicator of your own internal pressures and fears. Be aware whether your thoughts are driving you, in which case they may be driving the pupil, causing him considerable discomfort and distress. Or whether they are undermining you: *"I'll never be able to teach this"*; or making you too relaxed: *"It's up to him"*, in which case the pupil may be feeling helpless: *"I'll never be able to learn this"*.
- The imagery behind every word you say to the pupil, as an indicator of your own feeling, which may be sensed by the pupil.
- Any lack of energy: any time in which your energy is not mutually harnessed, or in which the pupil's energy is not positively harnessed to his work.

Questionnaires

Design a questionnaire to ask pupils whatever you are interested in finding out, but remembering to keep questions related to the research and the results you hope to see. The shorter and simpler the question the better. For example:

"What would you like to achieve this term?"

"What are your ambitions for this year?"

"What are your ambitions for your whole music education?"

"What do you like about your lessons?"

"What do you dislike or dread?"

"What suggestions do you have for your lessons?"

Questions that could be answered "Yes" or "No" (or "Always" or "Never"), but where there are shades of grey, could be answered on a five-point scale where "1" indicates total satisfaction and "5" dissatisfaction. In this way the pupil may then feel he can record "3", to indicate negative experience, without unduly upsetting the teacher's feelings.

Questionnaires, by their comparative impersonality, are more likely to produce accurate replies than face-to-face questioning, but besides any deference to the teacher's feelings, we need to be aware of other possible bias which might result in the pupil not expressing himself accurately. These are:

- Ideal-Self bias (the pupil says what he'd like to believe about himself)
- Social-Desirability bias (the pupil says whatever will make him popular)
- Situational-Demand bias (the pupil says what feels right given the situation).

The teacher's own knowledge of and sensitivity towards the pupil can enable her to see the truth behind the answers. But in any event, questionnaires provide a useful starting point for discussion, particularly if the teacher remains helpfully disposed towards the pupil, and resolutely refuses to feel threatened by any discovery that previous lessons were not quite perfect!

Pupils and parent's reports

Ask pupils and/or parents to write a report of their experiences during the action research, noting in particular any positive outcomes.

Do the Research

When you begin your research you may find that it goes exactly as you anticipated, or you may not: You may find that your pupils are not responding, or that you are not getting the results you had expected or that something else completely unexpected happens. In any of these cases you may feel that you want to make adjustments to your method. You should feel free to make any such adjustments, but you must be clear and ready to explain why you are making them and what they are. Your own reflective process as a teacher-researcher and your ability to make appropriate adaptations in your teaching, are every bit as useful and important as your results.

Write up your Results

The results should show evidence of enhanced teaching and learning in the areas specified. They should also show evidence of your own reflective process during the research.

Draw your Conclusions and make Recommendations for further study

The conclusions and recommendations for further study should show evidence of your own reflective process.

Example of a Teacher's Plan for Action Research

Topic: Teaching Styles

Pupils: Three contrasting pupils

Clare, aged 8, (quick and capable)

John, aged 12, (likes music but slower and has dyslexia)

Christine, aged 16, (quite capable but doesn't often practise and could make more progress)

Aims: To experiment with pupil-directed lessons to see if they result in enhancing the quality of energy in the lesson and in the pupils practising more.

Method: Over a three-week period (three lessons per pupil) to experiment with pupil-directed learning as follows:

- Explain to the pupils that I would like to experiment with pupil-directed lessons to see if they are better than the lessons they are used to having. Ask the pupils if they would be happy to participate in this for three weeks and give feedback both during and after, through questionnaires, by talking and by a final, short report.
- Ask parents for permission and for their participation in writing a report of their observations at the end.
- Explain to pupils that they are to take charge of their own lessons deciding what to learn and how to learn. I will only help them if they ask for help. However, as the aim is to *enhance* lessons and practice I will feel free to modify pupil-direction with teacher-direction if it doesn't work well (if perhaps they start feeling lost and helpless as outlined in the book).
- Video the first and last lesson for each pupil.
- Use a self-awareness note book to jot down feelings and thoughts while teaching for later reflection.
- Have the pupils fill in a pre-prepared questionnaire (see overleaf) at the beginning and at the end of the research.
- Collect the pupils' and parents' reports.

Results: Collect and collate data from the video observation, the self-awareness note book, the pupils' questionnaires and the pupils' and parents' reports.

Conclusions and Recommendations:

Draw conclusions and make recommendations for further study.

The Questionnaire

To be given to each pupil twice: The first time at the beginning of the research in response to lessons up to that point (teacher-directed lessons), the second time at the end of the project in response to the three researched lessons experimenting with pupil-direction. The last three questions on the questionnaire are only to be answered the second time the questionnaire is given.

Pupil's Name.......................................

Answer briefly:

What was your favourite thing about these lessons?

What else gave you positive feelings in these lessons?

What did you least like in these lessons?

What else gave you negative feelings?

How much did you practise (average time per week)?

On a five-point scale: 1 is Always; 2 Usually; 3 Half of the time; 4 Rarely; 5 Never:

Did you like your lessons?

Did you look forward to your lessons?

Was your teacher empathetic?

Was your teacher helpful?

Did you feel you wanted to practise?

What did you enjoy practising?

At the end of the project only:

Do you prefer the lessons you had three weeks ago or your lessons now?

Is there anything you would like to add?

What suggestions do you have for these lessons?

THANK YOU FOR HELPING!

Afterword

I hope, above all, that this book has confirmed you in your own intuition, and helped you to use your intuition and skills, whether in teaching, learning or performing, with increased conscious intent to greater effect.

If you would like to share any feedback I would be very interested to hear from you at the e-mail address below.

If you would like to be put on the emailing list to receive information about courses in Practical Psychology, Playing by Ear and Improvising or Dance for musicians, please visit www.lucinda-mackworth-young.co.uk or email lucinda@lucinda-mackworth-young.co.uk.

References and Recommended Reading

Psychology and Emotions in Teaching and Learning

Derville, L. (1966) The Use of Psychology in Teaching London: Longman Group Ltd

Goleman, Daniel (1996) Emotional Intelligence: Why it can matter more than I.Q London: Bloomsbury

Holt, John (1965) How Children Fail Harmondsworth: Penguin Books Ltd.

Purkey, William W. (1976) Self concept and School Achievement New Jersey: Prentice-Hall Inc.

Rogers, Carl. (1969) Freedom to Learn Columbus, Ohio: Charles E.Merrill Publishing Co.

Saltzberger-Wittenberg, Isca, Henry, Gianna, and Osborne, Elsie. (1983) The Emotional Experience of Learning and Teaching London: Routledge and Kegan Paul plc.

Psychology, Child Development and Learning Strategies

Dennison, Paul E. (1986) Brain Gym and others from Edu-K Foundation U.K.

Gardner, Howard (1983) Frames of Mind: The Theory of Multiple Intelligences

Lansdown, Richard (1984) Child Development Made Simple London: William Heinemann Ltd

O'Connor, Joseph (1987) Not Pulling Strings London: Lambeth Books

Reay, David G. (1994) Understanding How People Learn London: Kogan Page Ltd.

Counselling/ Spiritual Psychology

Carter-Scott, Cherie (1998) If Life is a Game, These are the Rules London: Hodder and Stoughton

Charles, Rachel (2000) Your Mind's Eye London: Judy Piatkus Publishers

de Board Robert (1997) Counselling for Toads London: Routledge

Egan, Gerard and Bailey, Andrew (2000) TalkWorks at work Sponsored by BT FutureTalk product: www.bt.com/futuretalk

Glasser, William (1965) Reality Therapy New York: Harpers and Row

Harris, Thomas A. (1967) I'm OK You're OK New York: Harpers and Row

Kahn, Michael (1991) Between Therapist and Client U.S.A.: W.H.Freeman and Company

Kennedy, Eugene and Charles, Sara C. (1990) On Becoming a Counsellor Dublin: Gill and Macmillan

Redfield, James (1997) The Celestine Vision London: Bantam Press

Roth, Gabrielle (1995) Maps to Ecstasy London: Thorsons

Symos, Miriam, Starhawk (1989) The Spiral Dance New York: HarperCollins

Psychological/Educational/Musical Research

Davidson, J.W., Moore, D.G., Sloboda, J.A. and Howe, M.J.A. (1998) "Characteristics of music teachers and the progress of young instrumentalists" Journal of Research into Music Education, 46, 1, 141-160

Doyle, W. (1983) Academic Work. Review of Educational Research, 53, 2, 159-199

Gustafson, Ruth I. (1986) "Effects of interpersonal dynamics in the student-teacher dyads on diagnostic and remedial content of four private violin lessons". Psychology of Music, 14, 130-139

Ingram, John and Worrall, Norman (1987) "The negotiating classroom: Child self-determination in British Primary Schools". Early Child Development and Care Vol. 28, 409-423

Kroeker, Charlotte Y. (1981) The application of the Rogerian theory of learning to the teaching of piano in a higher educational setting. (Unpub. PhD.University of Kansas)

Mackworth-Young L. (1990) Pupil-centred learning in piano lessons: an evaluated action-research programme focusing on the psychology of the individual. Psychology of Music, 18, 73-86. This research is summarised in Music Teacher: 1990 April

Sloboda, J.A. and Howe, M.J.A. (1991) "Biographical precursors of musical excellence: An interview study". Psychology of Music, 19, 3-21

Instrumental Music Education

Hallam, Susan (1998) Instrumental Teaching Oxford: Heinemann

Harris, Paul and Crozier, Richard (2000)
The Music Teacher's Companion, A Practical Guide
London: The Associated Board of the Royal Schools of Music

Mackworth-Young L. (1992-99) Articles in Music Teacher: Rhinegold Publications Ltd
1992 June, August, October; 1994 October, December;
1995 February, April, June, August. 1999 April

Mackworth-Young L. (1999) Articles in Ensemble, The Journal for the MMA
1999 June, October

Shockley, Rebecca Payne (1997) Mapping Music: For Faster Learning and Secure Memory –A Guide for Piano Teachers and Students: USA A-R Editions, Inc.

Music, Movement and the Body

de Alacantara, Pedro (1997) Indirect Procedures, A Musicians Guide to the Alexander Technique: Oxford University Press

Feldenkrais, Moshe (1972) Awareness Through Movement London: Penguin Group

Harrison, Christine and Paull, Barbara (1997)
The Athletic Musician, a guide to playing without pain London: The Scarecrow Press

Haselbach, Barbara (1981) Music, Dance, Movement London: Schotts

Mead, Virginia Hoge (1994) Dalcroze Eurhythmics in Today's Music Classroom
New York: Schott

Vanderspar, Elizabeth (1984) Dalcroze Handbook: available from the Book Secretary of The Dalcroze Society: Patsy James, 01932 348754
4 Cheniston Close, West Byfleet, Surrey KT1 46DQ

Performance

Evans, Andrew (1994) The Secrets of Musical Confidence: Thorsons

Green, Barry with Gallwey, W.Timothy (1986-87)
The Inner Game of Music
London: Pan Books Ltd.

Grindea, Carola (1995) Tensions in the Performance of Music: A Symposium
London: Kahn and Averill

Mackworth-Young L. (Nov 1994) Article in Flourish! The Journal of Trinity College of Music: "Coping with Exam Nerves"

Mackworth-Young L. (May 1998) Article in Libretto, The Journal of The Associated Board of the Royal Schools of Music: Exam Nerves: the Inner Critic

Ristad, Eloise (1982) A Soprano on her Head, Utah: Real People Press

Special Needs

Alvin, J. and Warwick, A. (1978) Music Therapy for the Autistic Child

Oxford University Press

Oglethorpe, Sheila (1996) Instrumental Music for Dyslexics: A Handbook for Teachers London: Whurr Publications